EDEN WILDER

AI for Beginners

Master AI Learning With Easy-to-Understand Tool Selection, Hands-On Practice and Career Optimization Insights

First published by Self-Published 2024

First edition

ISBN (paperback): 978-1-0695585-5-8
ISBN (hardcover): 978-1-0695585-6-5

This book was professionally typeset on Reedsy.
Find out more at reedsy.com

Contents

Introduction

One morning, while waiting for your morning drink, you might pull out your phone and ask a voice assistant for the weather. Without much thought, you rely on this AI to guide your day. It's seamless and natural. Yet, behind this simple interaction lies a vast world of Artificial Intelligence, a realm often seen as complex and out of reach for many.

AI has crept into our everyday lives, quietly shaping how we interact with technology. From personalized recommendations on streaming platforms to automated emails sorting your inbox, AI is at work. It's fascinating, but for many, still a mystery. The sheer breadth of AI can feel intimidating, filled with jargon, and seemingly reserved for tech experts. This perception creates a gap—a barrier where there shouldn't be one, especially considering how much AI can enhance our lives.

The purpose of this book is to break down that barrier. I aim to demystify AI for you. My vision is simple: make AI accessible and valuable in everyday life. You don't need to be a coder or a tech guru to understand or benefit from AI. With the proper guidance, anyone can tap into its potential and improve personal and professional aspects of life.

Throughout this book, we will cover key topics to build your understanding. We will start with basic AI concepts, giving you a foundation. Then, we'll explore popular AI tools, like ChatGPT, which you can use for general purposes such as writing and scheduling. We'll look into AI applications in specialized fields like image creation, executive assistance, and even psychological help. Each chapter is designed to build on the last, gradually expanding your knowledge and confidence.

What makes this book unique is its focus on real-life applications. The explanations are beginner-friendly without diving into technical complexity. We will focus on practical knowledge and exercises so you can see immediate benefits. This sets the book apart from others, ensuring that tech barriers don't impede your learning journey.

Some of you may feel hesitant about AI. You might think it's too advanced or worry about its implications. This book addresses those concerns directly. It's crafted for seekers of the fundamentals, with curiosity as the only prerequisite. I encourage you to approach AI with an open mind, ready to explore its possibilities and challenges.

As you progress, you will gain practical skills and a broad understanding of AI's potential. We'll also touch on ethical considerations, discussing how AI impacts the job market and climate innovations. By the end, you will not only understand AI but feel empowered to use it effectively in your life.

In the end, this book aims to inspire and empower you. AI is not just a tool for experts; it's for everyone. By understanding and leveraging AI, you can enhance your life, streamline tasks, and explore new opportunities. Welcome to the journey. Let's begin.

1

Laying the Groundwork for AI

Have you ever wondered how your favorite streaming service seems to know precisely what you want to watch next or how your smartphone can understand your voice commands with surprising accuracy? These conveniences, which we often take for granted, are powered by Artificial Intelligence, a technology that has quietly woven itself into the fabric of our daily routines. Consider the last time you asked Siri for directions or had Alexa play your favorite song. These virtual assistants are more than just cool gadgets; they are manifestations of AI, demonstrating its potential to simplify tasks and enhance our lives. Yet, for many, the concept of AI remains shrouded in complexity and mystique, making it seem like an exclusive domain for tech experts. This chapter aims to strip away that mystique and lay a clear foundation for understanding AI without the intimidating jargon.

1.1 What is AI? An Introduction Without the Jargon

At its core, Artificial Intelligence is about machines performing tasks that typically require human intelligence. Think of it as teaching computers to mimic how we think and solve problems. AI can analyze data, recognize patterns, and make decisions based on the information it receives, much like our brains do. It powers everything from smart home devices to sophisticated search engines, quietly working behind the scenes to make technology more intuitive and responsive.

Virtual assistants like Siri and Alexa are prime examples of AI in action. They understand spoken language, process it, and deliver responses that match our queries. This capability resembles our cognitive functions, where we listen, process, and respond. These systems learn from interactions and improve over time, making each experience with them better than the last. This adaptability sets AI apart from traditional software, which follows a fixed set of rules and lacks the ability to learn or adapt.

Traditional software operates on predetermined logic, where you must explicitly define every possible scenario the software might encounter. It's like setting a thermostat to a fixed temperature: it follows instructions without deviation. In contrast, AI systems are dynamic. They are designed to learn from data, adapt to new information and improve their performance over time. This self-learning capability allows AI applications to handle complex tasks remarkably efficiently and flexibly. For instance, think of a music recommendation service that evolves based on your listening habits, suggesting new artists and genres as it learns your preferences—a feat traditional programming would struggle to achieve.

Despite its capabilities, AI is often surrounded by misconceptions. One common fear is that AI will ultimately replace human jobs. While AI does automate specific tasks, it also creates new opportunities, enabling us to focus on creative and strategic roles that require a human touch. Consider how AI helps in medical diagnostics, allowing doctors to spend more time with patients by quickly analyzing complex data. Instead of replacing jobs, AI shifts the focus, enhancing what we can achieve together with technology.

Another myth is that AI will eventually become sentient, developing human-like consciousness. This notion, often fueled by science fiction, is far from reality. Current AI systems lack self-awareness; they operate based on algorithms and data without understanding or emotions. They excel at specific tasks but don't possess the general intelligence or consciousness that defines human thought. Understanding this distinction helps demystify AI, making it more approachable and less intimidating.

By recognizing AI's practical applications and dispelling myths, you can appreciate its role in everyday life. AI is not just a tool for scientists or tech enthusiasts; it's a resource for everyone, designed to enhance daily experiences and streamline tasks. The purpose of this chapter, and indeed this book, is to demystify AI and provide you with the knowledge and skills to navigate this exciting field confidently. With an open mind and a willingness to explore, you'll discover that AI can be both accessible and empowering, offering endless possibilities for personal and professional growth.

1.2 Key AI Terminologies Explained

When diving into the world of AI, you'll encounter a set of terms that form the basics of understanding how this technology functions. Consider the algorithm, essentially a set of rules or a process a computer follows to solve a problem. In AI, algorithms guide systems to make decisions or predictions based on input data. They are the fundamental building blocks upon which AI operates, directing the system's actions like a GPS does for a driver. Algorithms in AI are crafted to handle complex tasks, processing vast amounts of data to derive insights or automate processes. While the term may sound technical, at its heart, an algorithm is an organized way to solve a problem, just like following steps to assemble a piece of furniture.

Machine Learning, often abbreviated as ML, takes this concept further by allowing systems to learn from data rather than being explicitly programmed for every scenario. Imagine teaching a child to recognize animals. Initially, you show pictures and names; over time, they start identifying animals on their own. This is similar to how machine learning works. It involves feeding data into an AI system to identify patterns and make predictions. Unlike traditional programs, which require specific instructions, machine learning algorithms adapt. They improve as they process more data, becoming better at tasks like predicting stock market trends or recommending products based on past purchases. This ability to learn and adapt makes machine learning a cornerstone of AI, powering everything from spam filters in your email to voice recognition systems in your phone.

A neural network, meanwhile, is a more advanced concept inspired by the human brain's structure and function. Visualize a network of neurons communicating with each other to process information—this is the biological inspiration behind neural networks. In AI, these networks consist of layers of interconnected nodes, or artificial neurons, that work together to analyze data. Each node processes input and transmits information to other nodes, mimicking how neurons communicate. This setup allows neural networks to recognize patterns, even in complex datasets, making them invaluable for tasks like image recognition and natural language processing. These networks are foundational for large models like those powering virtual assistants and chatbots, enabling them to understand and generate human-like responses.

When it comes to jargon or slang, neural networks are often described as deep learning systems. Picture a stack of pancakes, where each layer adds more depth and flavor. Similarly, in deep learning, each layer of the network processes data at a different level of abstraction, allowing the system to understand complex features. This layered approach enables deep learning models to handle intricate tasks, like distinguishing between different breeds of dogs in photos or translating languages in real-time. Deep learning's strength lies in its ability to process raw data, such as images or audio, and extract meaningful insights without manual feature engineering. This is why deep learning models have become the standard for handling large, unstructured datasets.

Exercise: Exploring AI Terms

To deepen your understanding, take a moment to reflect on how you've interacted with AI without realizing it. Think about an app or service you use regularly, like a streaming platform or a virtual assistant, and consider the algorithmic decisions that enhance your experience. Jot down your thoughts on how these interactions rely on machine learning or neural networks. Reflecting on these everyday experiences helps demystify AI and shows its practical applications in your life.

Understanding these foundational terms is crucial as they form the language of AI discussions. Algorithms, machine learning, and neural networks represent the core components driving AI innovations, each playing a distinct role in making systems smarter and more effective. We bridge the gap between complex technology and everyday understanding by breaking down these concepts into relatable analogies. As you continue to explore AI, keep these terms in mind—they are the keys to unlocking how AI shapes the world around us.

1.3 Understanding Algorithms: The Basics You Need to Know

The functioning of algorithms in AI can be similar to following a recipe: you gather ingredients, follow each step, and end up with a delicious result. At their core, algorithms are sets of instructions that guide machines to solve problems or perform tasks. They are the recipes that computers follow to process information, make decisions, and deliver outcomes. In the realm of AI, algorithms are indispensable. They form the backbone of decision-making processes, enabling machines to process data, identify patterns, and execute tasks efficiently. Whether it's sorting your emails, recommending a new show, or even diagnosing medical conditions, algorithms are at work behind the scenes, tirelessly executing sequences to achieve desired results.

The beauty of AI algorithms lies in their ability to learn and adapt. Unlike static instructions that remain unchanged, AI algorithms evolve by interacting with data. Consider a streaming service that recommends movies. Initially, it might base suggestions on popular titles, but over time, as it gathers more information about your preferences, it refines recommendations to match your tastes better. This learning process involves feeding the algorithm with training data—a collection of examples that help it understand what works and what doesn't. As it processes this data, the algorithm refines its model, improving its accuracy and effectiveness. It's akin to a musician practicing scales until they can play a complex piece effortlessly. The more data the algorithm encounters, the better it becomes at predicting and responding to new inputs, making it a dynamic and adaptable tool.

Real-world applications of learning algorithms are abundant. Take recommendation systems, for instance. These systems analyze user behavior to suggest products, music, or articles that align with individual preferences. By examining past interactions, such as previous purchases or browsing history, the algorithm identifies patterns and predicts future interests. In essence, it becomes a personalized assistant, fine-tuning its suggestions to cater to unique tastes. The power of such systems lies in their ability to enhance user experience, making interactions more relevant, engaging, and efficient. They transform vast amounts of data into actionable insights, adding value to everyday activities and decisions.

However, developing effective algorithms comes with its own set of challenges. One significant hurdle is ensuring data quality and addressing bias. Algorithms are only as good as the data they process. If the input data is flawed, incomplete, or biased, the algorithm's output will reflect these deficiencies, leading to skewed or inaccurate results. For instance, if an algorithm designed to screen job applicants is trained on biased data, it may unfairly favor certain candidates over others, perpetuating existing inequalities. Achieving high-quality data requires meticulous collection and preprocessing, ensuring that algorithms operate fairly and accurately. It involves scrutinizing datasets for errors, inconsistencies, and biases and making necessary adjustments to maintain objectivity and reliability.

Another challenge is the requirement for substantial computational power. Training complex algorithms, particularly those involved in deep learning, demands significant processing capabilities. The intricate computations and vast datasets involved necessitate advanced hardware and efficient algorithms to achieve timely results. This need for resources can be a barrier for smaller organizations or individuals, limiting their ability to leverage AI's full potential. It emphasizes the importance of optimizing algorithms for both performance and efficiency, balancing their complexity with practical considerations such as execution speed and resource consumption.

Despite these challenges, the development and refinement of algorithms continue to drive AI's transformative impact across various industries. From healthcare to finance, entertainment to education, algorithms are reshaping how we interact with technology and how technology interacts with us. They empower machines to think, adapt, and assist in ways previously unimaginable, opening doors to new possibilities and innovations. As we continue to explore AI's potential, understanding the intricacies and capabilities of algorithms is crucial. They are the engines that power AI applications, driving progress and enabling machines to perform tasks with unprecedented precision and intelligence. Through careful design, testing, and iteration, algorithms unlock the power of AI, transforming ideas into reality and paving the way for a future enriched by intelligent systems.

1.4 From Data to Insight: How AI Learns from Information

Data is essential for the functionality of AI systems, similar to how fuel is necessary for a car to operate. Without sufficient data, AI cannot perform its tasks effectively. Whether it's recognizing faces in a crowded room or predicting weather patterns, AI relies on vast amounts of data to function. This data comes in many forms—images, text, numbers—and is gathered from various sources like social media, sensors, or financial records. However, raw data is rarely in a ready-to-use form. It often requires extensive preprocessing, like cleaning and preparing ingredients before cooking. This involves collecting data from reliable sources and ensuring it's accurate and relevant. Preprocessing might also involve normalizing data, which means adjusting values measured on different scales to a common scale. This step is crucial because it ensures that the AI models interpret the data correctly, leading to more accurate outcomes.

Once data is preprocessed, it enters the realm of data processing techniques, where AI systems extract meaningful features. Feature extraction is the process of identifying key characteristics within the data that are essential for making predictions. Imagine trying to recognize a friend in a crowd; you wouldn't focus on every single detail but rather on distinct features like their hairstyle or clothing. Similarly, AI systems identify relevant features that distinguish one piece of data from another. This could involve recognizing edges in an image or specific words in a text document. By focusing on these features, AI can make sense of complex data and distill it into something more manageable and valuable.

This process is supported by data cleaning, which involves removing duplicates, correcting errors, and filling in missing values to ensure the data's integrity.

With data processed and features extracted, AI systems can transform this raw information into actionable insights. Pattern recognition is one of the primary ways AI achieves this, identifying trends and regularities within the data. For instance, in healthcare, AI might recognize patterns in patient records indicating early signs of a disease, prompting timely intervention. Similarly, anomaly detection allows AI to spot deviations from the norm, which can be crucial in fields like finance for identifying fraudulent transactions. Predictive analytics takes these insights a step further, using historical data to forecast future events. Businesses use predictive analytics to anticipate consumer behavior, optimize supply chains, or even prevent equipment failures by predicting maintenance needs. In healthcare, predictive models can foretell patient outcomes or the spread of diseases, aiding doctors in making informed decisions.

Despite these transformative capabilities, the use of data in AI is not without its challenges and ethical considerations. One of the major concerns is privacy. As AI systems require large amounts of data to function, ensuring that this data is used ethically and securely becomes paramount. Unauthorized access or misuse of personal data can have serious repercussions, leading to breaches of privacy and trust. This is why stringent data protection measures and regulations, such as the GDPR in Europe, are in place to safeguard individuals' information. Beyond privacy, data bias poses another significant challenge. If the data used to train AI systems is biased, the outcomes will reflect these biases, leading to unfair or discriminatory results. For instance, a biased dataset in a hiring algorithm might favor certain demographics over others, perpetuating existing inequalities. Addressing these biases involves careful examination of the data and implementing corrective measures to ensure fairness and objectivity.

Navigating these challenges requires a balanced approach, where data is used responsibly to harness AI's potential while respecting individual rights and societal norms. The journey from raw data to actionable insight is complex, involving meticulous steps to ensure accuracy, relevance, and ethical integrity. As AI continues to evolve, the role of data will only grow more critical, opening new avenues for innovation across diverse fields. By understanding these processes, we can appreciate how AI transforms data into powerful insights, driving advancements that enhance our daily lives and the world at large.

1.5 AI in Everyday Life: Practical Examples

Nowadays, customer service interactions are often automated with chatbots, especially during late-night hours. Instead of waiting for a human representative, customers can receive immediate assistance from AI-powered systems. This trend is becoming more prevalent as businesses adopt AI to improve their communication efficiency. Chatbots, driven by complex algorithms, can handle various customer queries, freeing human agents for more nuanced tasks. This efficiency is crucial for businesses aiming to provide 24/7 support, and it benefits customers by offering immediate assistance. AI-driven language translation tools also break down language barriers, facilitating communication across different cultures. These tools, which translate text and speech almost instantaneously, enable seamless global interactions, be it for travel, business, or personal connections. The capacity to communicate effortlessly in multiple languages enriches our interactions, making the world seem a bit smaller and more connected.

In our personal lives, AI has taken on the role of a virtual assistant, seamlessly integrating into our daily routines. Consider smart home devices that adjust lighting, regulate temperature, or even brew your morning coffee at a simple voice command. These devices use AI to learn your habits and preferences, creating a personalized environment that enhances comfort and convenience. Similarly, AI-powered scheduling apps organize your day, manage appointments, and send reminders, ensuring you stay on track and maximize productivity. They analyze your calendar, suggesting optimal times for meetings or breaks, adapting as your day unfolds. This level of automation not only saves time but also reduces stress, allowing you to focus on tasks that require your full attention.

AI's influence extends to entertainment and media, transforming how we consume content. Streaming services rely on AI to recommend shows and movies, tailoring suggestions to your viewing habits. By analyzing what you've watched and liked, these platforms present options you're likely to enjoy, often introducing you to new genres or directors. This personalization enhances your viewing experience, ensuring you spend more time enjoying content rather than searching for it. Beyond recommendations, AI generates content, from music compositions to articles, expanding the creative possibilities. Musicians and writers use AI tools to collaborate on projects, experimenting with new styles and ideas that push the boundaries of their art. This collaboration between human creativity and AI innovation results in unique, diverse offerings that enrich cultural landscapes.

The realm of health and wellness is another area where AI is making significant strides. Personalized fitness apps powered by AI design workout routines tailored to your fitness level and goals. These apps track progress, adjust exercises, and provide real-time feedback, acting as virtual trainers. This accessibility encourages healthier lifestyles, making fitness routines adaptable and achievable for everyone. In the mental health sector, AI supports therapists by offering preliminary assessments and ongoing monitoring. Chatbots or apps provide a platform for individuals to express concerns, receive advice, or practice mindfulness techniques. While not a substitute for professional care, these tools offer supplementary support, making mental health resources more accessible and reducing stigma.

These examples illustrate how deeply AI is embedded in our daily lives, often in ways we might not immediately recognize. Its integration into communication, personal assistance, entertainment, and wellness highlights its versatility and potential to enhance various aspects of life. By simplifying tasks, enriching experiences, and supporting well-being, AI has proven itself a valuable ally in navigating the complexities of modern living. However, as we embrace these advancements, it's important to remain mindful of the ethical and societal implications. Balancing innovation with responsibility ensures that AI continues to serve humanity positively and equitably. As you continue exploring AI, consider how these technologies might further evolve, shaping the future in ways yet to be imagined.

2

Navigating AI Tools and Platforms

Imagine walking into a bustling marketplace where each stall offers a unique tool designed to make life a little easier. This marketplace represents the world of AI tools, each promising to enhance productivity, creativity, or simply add convenience to your day. But, like any market, the sheer number of options can be overwhelming, especially when you're just starting. You might wonder which tool fits your needs or how to even begin choosing. This chapter is here to guide you through this complex landscape, helping you understand what to look for and how to make informed decisions.

2.1 Choosing the Right AI Tools: A Beginner's Guide

The first step in selecting the perfect AI tool is understanding what you need it for. Consider whether your interest is personal or professional. Are you looking to streamline your daily tasks, such as organizing your schedule or managing emails? Or are you exploring AI for career-related goals, perhaps to improve your presentations or boost your team's productivity? Defining your purpose will narrow down the options significantly. Also, keep in mind your budget constraints. Many AI tools come with free versions, but some of the more advanced features might require a subscription. Balancing your requirements with what you're willing to spend is crucial in making a choice that satisfies both your functional and financial needs.

Once you've identified your needs, it's time to delve into the features and capabilities of potential AI tools. The user interface is an essential consideration—look for tools that offer intuitive and straightforward navigation. This ease of use ensures that you can quickly adapt to the tool without extensive training. Additionally, check for compatibility with your existing devices and software. A tool that seamlessly integrates with what you already use will enhance efficiency rather than create extra work. Understanding these elements helps in selecting a tool that not only meets your needs but also fits smoothly into your current workflow.

With a clearer understanding of your needs and desired features, you can now evaluate popular AI tools available on the market. It's helpful to compare free versus paid versions to see which offers the best value for your needs. Free tools can be a great starting point, providing basic features that allow you to explore the tool's potential. However, if you find a particular tool indispensable, investing in a paid version might unlock additional functionalities that enhance your experience. Customer reviews and ratings are invaluable resources at this stage. They provide insights into real-world usage and can highlight any potential issues you might have yet to consider.

Armed with this information, making an informed decision becomes more manageable. Take advantage of trial periods and demos offered by many AI tools. These allow you to experiment with the tool's features firsthand, providing a better sense of its utility before committing financially. Additionally, consulting with peers or colleagues who have experience with similar tools can offer practical insights. They might suggest alternatives you hadn't considered or share tips on maximizing the tool's effectiveness. Their firsthand knowledge can be an excellent complement to your research, helping you feel more confident in your choice.

Checklist: Choosing Your First AI Tool

- *Define your primary need: personal or professional?*
- *Set a realistic budget for AI investments.*
- *Identify key features and ensure ease of use.*
- *Verify compatibility with current devices and software.*
- *Compare free and paid versions for value.*
- *Read customer reviews for genuine feedback.*
- *Utilize trial periods to test tools.*
- *Seek recommendations from experienced peers.*

Taking these steps will not only make the process of choosing an AI tool less daunting, but also ensure that you select a tool that truly enhances your productivity and creativity.

2.2 Getting Started with ChatGPT for Everyday Tasks

ChatGPT is a digital assistant that facilitates communication and helps users organize their daily tasks. It is a conversational AI created to enhance task management through straightforward interactions. At its core, ChatGPT operates as a chatbot capable of understanding and responding to natural language inputs. It retrieves information, answers questions, and even engages in casual conversation. Its ability to automate tasks through scripts and prompts makes it a versatile tool for managing your day-to-day activities. Whether you're drafting emails or brainstorming ideas for your next project, ChatGPT is like having an assistant who's always ready to help, responding to your queries with remarkable speed and accuracy.

Setting up ChatGPT is straightforward, and designed with user-friendliness in mind. Begin by creating an account on the platform hosting ChatGPT, like OpenAI or another service offering its integration. The sign-up process typically involves providing an email address and setting a password. Once registered, you can access the platform via a web interface or a dedicated app, depending on your preference. Upon logging in, you'll be greeted with a user-friendly dashboard where you can configure basic settings. This might include selecting preferred languages, customizing response styles, or setting up specific prompts for automation. Such customization ensures ChatGPT works in a way that suits your personal or professional needs, making interactions more productive and enjoyable.

Think of all the small tasks that fill your day—responding to emails, setting reminders, or seeking inspiration for new projects. ChatGPT can handle these efficiently, freeing up time for more critical activities. For instance, when drafting emails, you can provide ChatGPT with key points. It will then craft a coherent message, ready for your review. It also helps manage communications by sorting through emails, highlighting important ones, and even suggesting responses. Beyond email, ChatGPT can serve as a brainstorming partner. Stuck on a project? Pose a question or share a challenge, and ChatGPT will generate ideas or suggest strategies, sparking creativity and moving your project forward.

Of course, like any tool, ChatGPT has its quirks, and users may occasionally encounter issues. Sometimes, the responses might not hit the mark, either due to misunderstanding the query or providing generic answers. To address inaccuracies, try rephrasing your question or providing more context. This helps the AI understand your intent better. Another common issue is managing conversation context, especially in longer interactions where the AI might lose track of the topic. To mitigate this, keep prompts clear and concise, resetting the context when necessary to maintain focus. These simple troubleshooting steps can enhance your experience, ensuring that ChatGPT remains a helpful and reliable assistant.

2.3 Image Creation with AI: Tools for Creative Projects

Artificial intelligence can assist in the creative process by providing tools that help generate art based on user inputs. It transforms creative ideas into visual representations, allowing for the realization of artistic concepts. Today, AI tools like Canva AI, DeepArt, and DALL-E are revolutionizing the way we create digital images. Canva AI, available with the Pro version of Canva and a favorite among designers, offers a plethora of design templates that simplify the creative process. Whether you're crafting a social media post or designing a flyer, Canva AI's intuitive interface and vast library of customizable templates make it accessible to users at all skill levels. It's like having a personal design team at your fingertips, ready to assist with every creative whim.

DeepArt, on the other hand, takes image creation a step further by enabling artistic transformations. This tool allows you to apply the techniques of famous artists to your own photos, creating unique pieces that blend technology with traditional art styles. Imagine transforming a simple photograph into a painting reminiscent of Van Gogh or Monet. DeepArt uses neural networks to analyze the style of any given artwork and replicate it in your image, creating a fusion of creativity and technology that is both stunning and innovative. It's perfect for those who wish to explore the boundaries of digital artistry without needing extensive artistic training.

Then there's DALL-E by OpenAI, which offers an entirely new dimension of possibilities. Unlike traditional image editors, DALL-E generates images from textual descriptions. This means you can simply type what you envision, and DALL-E will create it for you. Want a picture of a two-headed flamingo standing in a field of tulips? Just describe it, and DALL-E brings it to life. The tool's ability to understand and interpret textual prompts into visual content opens up endless creative opportunities, letting your imagination run wild without the limitations of manual drawing or editing skills.

Creating digital art with these AI tools begins with selecting styles and templates that match your vision. For instance, in Canva AI, you start by choosing a template that suits your project—be it a business card or an Instagram story. From there, you can adjust parameters like color schemes, fonts, and layouts to create a personalized design that aligns with your brand or aesthetic. DeepArt requires you to upload an image and choose an artistic style to transform it, allowing you to experiment with different effects until you achieve the desired outcome. DALL-E's process is even more straightforward: you input a descriptive sentence, and the AI handles the rest, generating an image that reflects your imagination.

In professional settings, AI-generated images play a crucial role in design and marketing. Businesses use these tools to quickly and efficiently create visually appealing marketing materials, such as brochures, posters, and online advertisements. The ability to design professional-grade visuals without a background in graphic design saves time and resources, allowing companies to focus on their core activities. Similarly, social media content creators leverage AI to design eye-catching graphics that engage audiences and enhance their online presence. The speed and ease with which AI tools generate high-quality visuals make them indispensable in a fast-paced digital world where captivating visuals are vital to capturing attention.

Collaborating on AI-created art is as straightforward as sharing a link. Many AI tools offer cloud-based platforms where you can store your creations, making it easy to share and collaborate with others. For instance, Canva AI allows you to export your designs in various formats, perfect for printing or sharing digitally. You can also invite colleagues or friends to collaborate directly within the platform, offering real-time editing and feedback. This facilitates creative teamwork, enabling multiple contributors to refine a project simultaneously. Whether you're printing a piece for a gallery exhibit or posting on social media, AI makes it easy to distribute and showcase your work to a broad audience.

2.4 AI for Time Management: Utilizing AI as an Executive Assistant

AI tools for time management and planning offer users a structured organization of their daily tasks, meetings, and goals. These tools can help improve scheduling efficiency and task prioritization, ultimately enhancing productivity in daily operations. Imagine finishing work early every day and having time for your personal life and projects. This is the promise of AI tools designed for time management and planning, transforming how you approach your daily schedule. Tools like Motion and Clockwise have become indispensable for those seeking to optimize their time effectively. Motion, for instance, helps manage your day with high visibility, allowing you to oversee tasks and projects seamlessly. Its AI-driven calendar integrates tasks automatically, ensuring you never miss a deadline. Clockwise, on the other hand, excels in syncing team calendars, making it perfect for those who work collaboratively. It learns from your habits, suggesting the best times for meetings and focused work, helping you maintain a balanced schedule. Integrations with Google Calendar mean these tools fit effortlessly into your existing routine, enhancing what you already use rather than replacing it.

Routine tasks often consume more time than we realize, but AI can automate these repetitive activities, freeing up valuable hours. Imagine setting up recurring events or appointments without manually inputting each one. AI tools can streamline this process, ensuring your calendar is always up-to-date with minimal intervention. Additionally, these tools can automatically generate to-do lists based on your emails and messages, capturing tasks you might otherwise overlook. This automation not only saves time but also reduces mental load, allowing you to focus on more pressing matters. For instance, an AI can scan your inbox and draft a list of action items, prioritizing them based on deadlines and importance. This capability transforms how you manage tasks, turning what was once a tedious chore into an efficient, automated process.

Boosting productivity involves more than just organizing tasks; it's about creating an environment that supports focus and efficiency. AI tools can help by prioritizing tasks according to deadlines, ensuring you tackle the most urgent items first. This prioritization helps prevent last-minute scrambles and reduces stress, as you always know what needs your immediate attention. Moreover, AI can block distractions by enabling focus modes that limit notifications and interruptions during critical work periods. This feature is particularly useful in maintaining concentration and flow, key components of productive work. By understanding your habits and preferences, AI tools can customize focus sessions, gently nudging you towards productive behavior without feeling intrusive or overly controlling.

Integrating AI tools into your personal workflows involves more than just adding another app to your phone; it's about finding harmony between technology and your work style. Syncing across multiple devices ensures that whether you're on a laptop, tablet, or smartphone, your schedule and tasks remain consistent and accessible. This seamless integration means you can switch devices without losing track of your day's plan. Additionally, AI tools facilitate team collaboration by providing shared calendars and task lists, ensuring everyone is aligned and informed. For example, when changes occur, like a meeting cancellation, the AI updates everyone involved, minimizing confusion and miscommunication. This collaborative feature is vital in dynamic environments where team members must adapt quickly to changes.

Interactive Exercise: Personalize Your AI Assistant

1. *Choose an AI tool like Motion or Clockwise.*
2. *Set up your daily schedule, including recurring tasks.*
3. *Enable focus modes during your peak productivity hours.*
4. *Sync with your team's calendars to enhance collaboration.*
5. *Reflect on the changes in your productivity after a week of use.*

By embracing these AI tools, you can transform your approach to time management, making each day more organized and productive. They offer not just a way to save time but a method to enhance the quality of how you spend it.

2.5 Writing with AI: Crafting Texts and Resumes

In today's digital landscape, AI writing assistants have become invaluable tools for anyone looking to enhance their writing skills. Whether you're drafting a report, composing an email, or polishing a resume, these AI-driven tools provide support and suggestions that can significantly improve the quality of your writing. Grammarly, for instance, acts as a vigilant proofreader, catching grammatical errors, suggesting stylistic improvements, and ensuring clarity. It offers real-time feedback, helping you maintain a professional tone in your communications. Hemingway, on the other hand, focuses on readability. It highlights complex sentences and suggests simpler alternatives, promoting concise and clear writing. These tools are like having an editor at your side, ready to refine your work with just a few clicks. For those who create content regularly, Jasper and Copy.ai offer advanced capabilities. They assist with generating ideas and drafting content, using AI to tailor the text to your specific needs, whether it's for marketing, blogging, or storytelling. These tools analyze your input and provide creative suggestions, helping to overcome writer's block and enhance your creativity.

Improving your writing with AI involves more than just correcting mistakes. These tools optimize your text for tone and clarity, ensuring that your message resonates with the audience. For example, when drafting an important email, AI can help adjust the tone to match the context, whether it's formal or casual. This ensures that your message is received as intended, reducing the risk of miscommunication. Additionally, by providing suggestions for sentence structure and word choice, AI tools help you develop a more engaging and effective writing style. This not only improves the quality of your work but also builds confidence in your writing ability. With practice, you'll notice an improvement in your writing skills, as AI tools encourage learning through their feedback.

When it comes to crafting a professional resume, AI can be a game-changer. Tools like Resumake and Resume.io offer a range of templates that cater to different industries and job roles. They guide you through the process of selecting a template that matches your career goals, ensuring a polished and professional appearance. But templates are just the starting point. AI tools also assist in highlighting your key achievements and skills, helping you present your experience in a way that stands out to employers. They analyze job descriptions and suggest keywords to include, optimizing your resume for applicant tracking systems. This makes your application more likely to reach human eyes, increasing your chances of landing an interview. With AI, resume writing becomes a strategic process where every element is tailored to maximize impact.

Beyond practical applications, AI also opens new avenues in creative writing. Imagine having a tool that helps you brainstorm plot ideas or develop characters for your novel. AI writing assistants can generate prompts based on your input, sparking inspiration when you're stuck. For instance, if you're developing a story, AI can suggest twists or character arcs that add depth to your narrative. This kind of support is invaluable for writers looking to explore new genres or styles. Moreover, AI can simulate dialogues, helping you create realistic interactions between characters. This feature is particularly useful for screenwriters and playwrights who need to craft engaging and believable conversations. By collaborating with AI, writers can push creative boundaries and experiment with new ideas, transforming the writing process into an exciting exploration of possibilities.

2.6 Psychological Help with AI: Exploring Emotional Support Tools

In recent years, AI has expanded beyond technical and creative realms, stepping into the delicate field of mental health. Imagine having a personal confidant available at any hour, ready to listen, offer support, and even help track your emotional well-being. AI applications like Woebot and Youper have been developed with this exact purpose in mind. These tools are designed to provide psychological support by engaging users in therapeutic conversations. Woebot, for example, uses cognitive-behavioral therapy principles to guide users through mood tracking and emotional journaling, gently nudging them towards healthier thinking patterns. Similarly, Youper uses AI to personalize interactions, offering mindfulness exercises and insights based on user input, making mental health support more accessible and immediate.

Another fascinating application is Replika, an AI that serves as a conversational partner, offering companionship and a safe space for users to express their thoughts and feelings. Replika adapts to the user's communication style, creating a unique and personal dialogue experience. This AI can help track mood changes over time, providing a record of emotional fluctuations that might otherwise go unnoticed. By identifying patterns and triggers, users can gain a better understanding of their emotional health. Moreover, these tools often include features that encourage mindfulness, providing exercises to calm the mind and enhance emotional awareness. Such practices can be beneficial in managing stress and maintaining mental balance.

However, as with any technology dealing with personal data, privacy and ethical considerations are paramount. Users must feel confident that their interactions are secure and confidential. These AI tools emphasize data security by encrypting conversations and storing information safely, ensuring that personal insights remain private. Developers follow ethical guidelines to protect user data, creating transparent privacy policies and consent forms. These measures are essential in building trust between users and AI, particularly in a field as sensitive as mental health. Ethical AI development involves ongoing evaluation and refinement to address potential biases and ensure fairness in interactions.

While AI tools offer valuable support, they are not a replacement for traditional therapy but rather a complement. Think of them as a bridge between therapy sessions, providing continuity and support when professional help isn't immediately available. AI can enhance therapy by offering insights gathered from interactions, which therapists might use to better understand their patient's needs and progress. By tracking emotions and behaviors, these tools provide additional context that can be discussed in therapy, enriching the therapeutic process. This synergy between AI and traditional therapy can lead to more personalized care, empowering individuals to take an active role in their mental health journey.

As you explore the world of AI tools for mental health, consider how they might fit into your routine or complement existing support systems. They represent a new frontier in emotional care, blending technology with empathy to provide innovative solutions for well-being. Embracing these tools can offer additional support and insight, enhancing your understanding of yourself and your mental health. As we move forward, the integration of AI into daily life continues to grow, offering more ways to connect, create, and care. This next chapter will explore how AI extends its reach into various specialized fields, including healthcare, robotics, and environmental solutions, showcasing its diverse applications and transformative potential.

3

Hands-On Practice with AI Tools

3.1 Interactive Exercises with ChatGPT

Imagine you're at a bustling café, listening to the lively chatter around you. Conversations flow effortlessly from one topic to another; each interaction is unique and dynamic. Now, picture your role in this setting, not as a passive observer but as an active participant, engaging with an AI conversational partner like ChatGPT. This AI doesn't just mimic human dialogue; it enhances it, becoming an integral part of your daily interactions. Welcome to the world where AI chatbots, like ChatGPT, offer a canvas for creativity and problem-solving, inviting you to explore its capabilities without needing any prior technical expertise. Whether you're simulating customer service exchanges or crafting stories with engaging dialogue, ChatGPT is your tool for interactive exercises that enhance your skills in a fun and accessible way.

To get started with ChatGPT, consider activities that tap into its conversational prowess. Begin by simulating customer service interactions, a common use case that highlights ChatGPT's ability to understand and respond to queries. Think about a typical customer service scenario, perhaps a customer inquiring about a product's return policy. You can set up ChatGPT to mimic this interaction by writing a prompt like, "A customer is asking about the return policy for a recently purchased item. Provide a detailed response, including any necessary steps." This exercise helps you practice crafting responses that are clear, concise, and customer-friendly. As you refine these interactions, you'll notice ChatGPT's adaptability, as it learns from your inputs and improves its responses, much like a well-trained customer service representative.

Another engaging way to use ChatGPT is by crafting dialogue for storytelling. Imagine you're writing a short story and need to develop a conversation between two characters. Provide ChatGPT with a prompt, such as, "Write a dialogue between a detective and a suspect in a mystery novel. The detective is trying to uncover details about a recent heist." This exercise encourages creativity and helps you explore different narrative styles and character voices. ChatGPT can offer diverse perspectives and plot twists, enriching your storytelling with unexpected depth. By engaging in these exercises, you enhance not only your writing skills, but also your ability to construct compelling narratives, an invaluable skill in any creative endeavor.

To make the most of ChatGPT, it's essential to understand how to write effective prompts. Start by being specific about the task or outcome you want to achieve. For example, instead of a vague request like "Tell me a story," specify the genre, setting, and characters involved. This specificity guides ChatGPT, enabling it to generate more relevant and coherent responses. Adjusting language model settings can further tailor the responses to your needs. You might want a humorous tone for a light-hearted story or a formal tone for professional interactions. Experiment with these settings to see how they influence ChatGPT's output, allowing you to find the right balance for each task.

As with any tool, you may encounter challenges while using ChatGPT. One common issue is handling ambiguous responses, where the AI struggles to interpret unclear prompts. To resolve this, try rephrasing your query or adding context to make your intentions clearer. If conversation flow becomes an issue, especially in longer dialogues where the AI might lose track of the topic, consider breaking the conversation into smaller, manageable parts. This approach maintains focus and ensures the dialogue progresses logically. Understanding these potential pitfalls and learning how to navigate them enhances your interactions with ChatGPT, making each session more productive and enjoyable.

Reflection Exercise: ChatGPT in Action

1. *Simulate a Customer Query: Create a scenario where a customer is curious about a new product launch. Use ChatGPT to draft a response that includes product features, benefits, and availability.*
2. *Craft a Dialogue: Write a prompt for a conversation between two historical figures meeting for the first time. Let ChatGPT take over, then refine the dialogue for accuracy and engagement.*
3. *Analyze and Adjust: Review the responses generated by ChatGPT. Identify areas for improvement and experiment with different prompts and settings to achieve the desired outcome.*

These exercises serve as a gateway to exploring creative use cases with ChatGPT. Beyond customer service and storytelling, consider brainstorming sessions where you use ChatGPT to generate ideas for your next project. By posing open-ended questions or challenges, you can tap into ChatGPT's ability to offer diverse perspectives, sparking inspiration and innovation. Similarly, ChatGPT can assist in developing interactive learning modules, providing explanations and quizzes that make educational content more engaging and accessible. As you continue to explore the possibilities, remember that ChatGPT is not just a tool but a partner in creativity, ready to expand your horizons and enhance your skills through practice and experimentation.

3.2 Creating Stunning Images with AI

AI image creation tools such as DALL-E and Artbreeder enable users to create visuals easily and efficiently. These tools significantly change the landscape of digital art by providing advanced capabilities to generate images with minimal effort. DALL-E, a tool available with ChatGPT Plus, is a tool that generates images from textual descriptions, allowing you to see your imagination come to life. Whether you envision a surreal landscape or a whimsical creature, DALL-E interprets your words into vibrant visuals. Artbreeder, on the other hand, is more collaborative, enabling you to blend and evolve images. Users can mix elements from different artworks, creating entirely new compositions by adjusting sliders that control various features.

To start creating images with DALL-E, begin by crafting a clear and detailed textual prompt. Describe what you want to see, including details like colors, styles, and specific objects. For example, you might write, "A sunset over a mountain range with purple clouds and a river flowing through the valley." Once you've crafted your prompt, enter it into DALL-E and let the AI do the rest. The tool generates several variations based on your description, each offering a unique interpretation. Review the outputs and select the one that best matches your vision, or iterate with new prompts to refine the result further.

With Artbreeder, the process involves selecting base images and experimenting with combinations. Start by choosing a primary image from the platform's extensive gallery. Then, select additional images to blend with the base. Artbreeder provides sliders to adjust features like color, texture, and composition, allowing you to experiment with different styles and effects. For instance, you might blend a portrait with a landscape, adjusting the sliders to create a harmonious fusion of the two. As you experiment, you can save iterations and share them with the Artbreeder community, gaining inspiration from the creations of others.

Personalizing your AI-generated images involves more than just selecting elements; it's about infusing your unique style into each piece. Both DALL-E and Artbreeder offer tools for adjusting color palettes and styles, giving you control over the visual tone of your work. In DALL-E, you can refine the color scheme by providing additional prompts or using editing software to tweak the final image. Artbreeder's sliders allow for real-time adjustments, enabling you to experiment with various palettes and textures until you achieve the desired effect. Incorporating personal elements, such as a signature motif or a recurring theme, can also make your creations truly yours.

AI image creation isn't just about replicating reality—it's a gateway to exploring new artistic styles and concepts. Consider using AI to create abstract art, where the goal is to evoke emotion rather than depict recognizable forms. Start with a simple prompt, like "an explosion of colors in the night sky," and see where the AI takes you. The results can be surprising and thought-provoking, pushing the boundaries of traditional art. Alternatively, use Artbreeder to design personalized digital artworks that reflect your interests and personality, such as custom avatars or fantasy landscapes.

Creative Prompt: Unlock Your Imagination

- Create an Abstract Piece: Use DALL-E to generate an abstract artwork. Begin with a vague prompt, such as "chaos in a dream-scape" and explore the results. Reflect on how the colors and shapes make you feel.

- Design a Unique Character: With Artbreeder, blend features from different portraits to create a character that could exist in a fictional universe. Adjust the details to match your vision, and

consider writing a short backstory for your creation.

AI image tools provide a playground for creativity, where the only limit is your imagination. They invite you to experiment, explore, and express without the constraints of traditional methods. Whether you're an aspiring artist or simply curious, these technologies offer an opportunity to engage with art in a new and exciting way.

3.3 AI-Powered Scheduling: A Practical Guide

Picture your day starting with a clear, organized schedule, all thanks to the magic of AI-powered scheduling tools like Motion. These tools are designed to streamline your life by handling the tedious but necessary task of managing your time. Setting up an AI scheduling tool is straightforward. Begin by downloading the app or accessing the web interface, and create an account using your email. Once you're in, the tool will guide you through an initial setup process. Here, you'll input your typical tasks, appointments, and deadlines. Most tools will ask you to connect your existing calendar, such as Google or Outlook, to sync events seamlessly. This integration allows the AI to assess your current scheduling habits and suggest improvements. During setup, you can also set your preferences for notifications and reminders, ensuring that you stay informed without feeling overwhelmed.

Creating and managing schedules with AI is a game-changer. Start by entering tasks and deadlines into the app. As you input these, the AI analyzes your entries, prioritizing them based on urgency and importance. For instance, if you have a meeting and a project deadline on the same day, the AI might suggest allocating more time to the project earlier in the day to ensure completion. This prioritization helps in balancing your workload efficiently. The AI's ability to adjust schedules on the fly is another advantage. Say an unexpected meeting pops up;

the AI can reshuffle your tasks, finding the best fit without you needing to adjust everything manually. This flexibility reduces stress, as you know your schedule is optimized to accommodate sudden changes while keeping your priorities intact.

The benefits of using AI for scheduling extend beyond just organization. One major advantage is the reduction of scheduling conflicts. By analyzing your calendar and understanding your preferences, the AI avoids double-booking and suggests optimal times for meetings that fit well into your existing commitments. This foresight is particularly beneficial when coordinating with teams, as the AI considers everyone's availability, proposing times that work best for all parties involved. Enhanced productivity is another key benefit. By intelligently managing your tasks, AI ensures you focus on what matters most at any given time. It can identify patterns in your work habits, suggesting breaks when you're most likely to be productive again, thus maintaining your efficiency throughout the day. These insights transform how you approach your workload, making your day more productive and less chaotic.

To maximize the effectiveness of your AI scheduling tool, regular updates to your task list are crucial. As new tasks arise, promptly add them to the tool to ensure your schedule remains current. This habit prevents last-minute rushes and keeps your workload balanced. Additionally, take time to review the AI-generated insights regularly. These insights often include suggestions for improving your time management, such as identifying peak productivity hours or recommending adjustments to your daily routine. By incorporating these suggestions, you can refine your scheduling habits, making informed decisions that enhance your efficiency. Also, don't hesitate to customize the tool's settings to fit your lifestyle better. Whether it's adjusting notification preferences or setting specific work hours, these tweaks ensure the tool aligns with your personal and professional needs, providing a tailored scheduling experience.

Engaging with AI-powered scheduling tools offers a unique opportunity to rethink how you manage your time. By embracing the capabilities of these tools, you invite a level of organization and efficiency that enhances both your personal and professional life. As you interact with the tool, you'll find that your days become more structured, your tasks more manageable, and your goals more attainable. This transformation doesn't require a drastic change in how you work; instead, it involves integrating a tool that complements your existing habits and amplifies your ability to achieve more with less effort. The process is intuitive, the benefits tangible, and the impact on your daily routine profound. Through this seamless integration, AI becomes an invaluable partner in navigating the complexities of modern life, offering a strategic approach to time management that keeps you ahead of the curve.

3.4 Crafting Resumes and Cover Letters with AI Assistance

Let's say you're about to apply for your dream job. The excitement is palpable, but so is the pressure to present yourself perfectly on paper. This is where AI writing tools come into play, transforming the daunting task of crafting resumes and cover letters into a streamlined, efficient process. With tools like Resume.io and Grammarly, you can create polished professional documents that stand out to potential employers. Resume.io offers an array of templates designed to cater to various industries and roles, making it easy to choose a format that aligns with your field. Its user-friendly interface guides you through each section, ensuring you include all the necessary details, from contact information to work experience. Meanwhile, Grammarly acts as your personal editor, meticulously combing through your text for grammatical errors and offering stylistic improvements. Together, these tools provide a solid foundation for showcasing your skills and achievements compellingly and accurately.

Creating a standout resume involves more than just listing your work history and skills. It requires thoughtful formatting and structuring to highlight your strengths effectively. Start by selecting a template from Resume.io that suits your industry. Consider elements like font style, layout, and color scheme, ensuring they reflect your professional brand. Once you've chosen a template, begin filling in your details. Start with a strong summary or objective statement that captures your career aspirations and what you bring to the table. Follow this with your work experience, listed in reverse chronological order. Be sure to include quantifiable achievements—numbers speak volumes in the eyes of recruiters. Next, detail your educational background and any relevant certifications or skills. Remember to tailor each section to the specific job you're applying for, emphasizing experiences and skills that align with the job description.

When it comes to cover letters, customization is key. A generic letter won't cut it in today's competitive job market. Use AI tools to draft a personalized cover letter that speaks directly to the role and company you're applying to. Start with a strong opening that grabs the reader's attention. Mention the position you're applying for and how you learned about the opportunity. In the body of the letter, highlight your most relevant experiences and skills, tying them to the job requirements. Use specific examples to demonstrate how you've successfully tackled similar challenges in the past. Conclude with a confident closing statement, expressing your enthusiasm for the role and your desire to contribute to the company. AI tools can help refine your language, ensuring your message is clear and persuasive while maintaining a professional tone.

While AI tools offer tremendous support in document creation, it's crucial to balance their input with your personal touch. Personalizing AI-generated content is essential to infuse your unique voice and experiences into the document. Use AI suggestions as a starting point, but make sure to tweak the language and examples to reflect your personality and career journey. Once your resume and cover letter are drafted, take the time to proofread them for accuracy and coherence. Grammarly can catch errors, but a human eye is invaluable for ensuring everything flows logically and reads smoothly. Consider asking a friend or mentor to review your documents—they might catch nuances that AI tools miss.

A personal tip: once your resume is completed, copy it into ChatGPT along with the job description and a prompt asking for a cover letter. This will allow the AI to write a cover letter based on your experiences and qualifications. You can modify or enhance it based on your preference, but the most significant part of the task will be handed to you.

AI-assisted writing has proven successful in real-world applications, with countless individuals leveraging these tools to secure interviews and job offers. For instance, consider the case of a recent college graduate who used Resume.io to create a visually appealing resume that highlighted her internship experiences and academic projects. The hiring manager at a prominent tech firm noticed her resume out of a pile of applicants, leading to an interview and ultimately a job offer. Similarly, a mid-career professional utilized Grammarly to craft a compelling cover letter for a managerial position, carefully matching the tone to the company's culture. Her attention to detail and tailored approach impressed the hiring committee, resulting in a successful career transition. These examples underscore the effectiveness of AI tools in enhancing professional documents helping applicants present themselves in the best possible light.

In the digital age, crafting resumes and cover letters with AI assistance is not just an option—it's a strategic advantage. By combining AI technology with your insights and experiences, you create documents that capture attention and convey your professional story effectively.

3.5 Exploring AI for Mental Health and Well-being

In a world where stress and anxiety are common, finding ways to manage mental health effectively has never been more crucial. AI tools are emerging as helpful allies in this endeavor, offering support and insights that can enhance your overall well-being. One such tool is Wysa, an AI-powered chatbot designed to track mood changes and provide emotional support. Think of Wysa as a virtual companion that listens without judgment, offering exercises and techniques to help you navigate your emotional landscape. By engaging with Wysa, you can gain a better understanding of your mood patterns and triggers, equipping yourself with strategies to handle life's ups and downs more effectively.

To dive into these AI mental health tools, start by setting up a virtual therapy assistant like Wysa on your smartphone. The installation process is straightforward: download the app, create an account, and complete a brief questionnaire to tailor the experience to your needs. Once set up, you can engage in daily conversations with the AI, which will guide you through exercises designed to improve your mental resilience. These exercises include breathing techniques, mindfulness practices, or even simple reflections on your day. By dedicating a few moments each day to these interactions, you cultivate a routine that fosters self-awareness and emotional balance.

Another valuable exercise involves using AI apps to track mood changes over time. These apps typically ask you to rate your mood at various points throughout the day, creating a digital journal of your emotional state. Over time, patterns emerge, revealing how different activities, interactions, or even times of day affect your mood. This information is invaluable, providing insights that can inform your decisions and help you manage stressors more effectively. The key is consistency—by regularly updating the app with your mood data, you build a comprehensive picture of your emotional health, empowering you to make informed adjustments to your lifestyle or routine.

As we embrace these innovative tools, it's essential to consider the ethical implications of using AI in mental health. Ensuring data privacy and security is paramount. These apps handle sensitive information, so it's crucial they employ robust encryption and have clear privacy policies. Always review these policies and understand how your data will be used and protected before engaging with any mental health AI tool. It's also important to maintain boundaries between AI and human support. While these tools offer valuable assistance, they are not substitutes for professional therapy. AI should complement, not replace, human interaction, providing support between therapy sessions or when professional help is not immediately accessible.

Incorporating AI into your well-being routine can be a simple yet powerful enhancement. Start by scheduling daily check-ins with your AI mood tracker. These brief sessions offer a moment of reflection, grounding you in the present and allowing you to assess your emotional state. Use these check-ins to set intentions for the day or reflect on achievements, no matter how small. Additionally, consider using AI reminders for mindfulness practices. Set an alert to prompt you to take a few minutes for deep breathing or meditation, helping you stay centered amidst the busyness of daily life. These small, consistent actions can have a significant impact on your mental health, promoting a sense of calm and well-being.

As we conclude this chapter, remember that AI tools are here to assist, not dictate. They offer guidance and support, but the real power lies in your hands. By integrating AI into your routines, you can enhance your self-care practices, gain valuable insights, and develop resilience. This journey of discovery is just beginning, with AI ready to support you every step of the way. As we transition to the next chapter, we will explore how AI continues to revolutionize industries, shaping the future in ways that are both exciting and transformative.

4

AI in Specialized Fields

4.1 AI in Healthcare: Innovations in the Medical Field

What if you're walking into a doctor's office where, instead of waiting for test results or relying solely on human interpretation, advanced AI systems are already hard at work, analyzing your medical data with precision and speed? This isn't science fiction; it's the reality of AI's role in modern healthcare. The integration of AI in medicine has transformed how we diagnose, treat, and manage health conditions, offering innovative solutions that enhance accuracy and efficiency. Picture an AI system examining an X-ray image, identifying subtle anomalies that might escape even the most trained eye, or envision machine learning models predicting the progression of diseases based on data patterns. These advancements represent a new era in diagnostics, where technology aids doctors in making quicker and more informed decisions, ultimately improving patient outcomes.

In the realm of diagnostics and imaging, AI has become an indispensable tool, enhancing the accuracy of medical diagnoses. Consider the process of examining X-rays and MRIs. Traditionally, radiologists scrutinize these images to detect abnormalities, a task that demands keen attention to detail. However, AI algorithms now augment this process, employing deep learning techniques to identify patterns and anomalies with remarkable precision. These algorithms can process vast amounts of imaging data swiftly, highlighting areas of concern and assisting radiologists in making accurate diagnoses. For instance, AI can detect early signs of tumors or fractures, enabling prompt intervention and treatment. The collaboration between human expertise and AI technology not only speeds up the diagnostic process but also reduces the risk of human error, ensuring patients receive the best possible care.

Beyond diagnostics, AI is reshaping personalized medicine and treatment plans, tailoring healthcare to individual needs. Imagine a scenario where AI-driven genetic analysis examines a cancer patient's unique genetic makeup to develop a personalized treatment plan. This approach, known as precision medicine, leverages AI to analyze genetic data, identifying specific mutations or biomarkers that influence disease progression. With this information, doctors can prescribe targeted therapies that are more effective and have fewer side effects. Similarly, predictive analytics play a crucial role in customizing medication regimens. AI models analyze patient data, predicting how individuals might respond to different treatments. This insight allows healthcare providers to optimize drug prescriptions, minimizing adverse reactions and maximizing therapeutic benefits. Through AI, medicine becomes more precise and personalized, offering hope for better health outcomes.

AI's influence extends to drug discovery and development, a field notorious for its complexity and cost. Traditionally, discovering new drugs involves years of research and substantial financial investment. However, AI accelerates this process by identifying potential drug candidates with unprecedented speed. Machine learning models sift through enormous datasets, pinpointing compounds that might have therapeutic potential. Once identified, AI simulates clinical trials, predicting outcomes and efficacy. This capability reduces the time and resources needed to bring new drugs to market, increasing the likelihood of discovering treatments for previously untreatable conditions. By streamlining drug development, AI not only drives innovation but also makes life-saving medications more accessible to patients worldwide.

The integration of AI in remote monitoring and telemedicine represents another frontier in healthcare innovation. Picture wearable AI devices that continuously track vital signs, providing real-time health data to patients and healthcare providers. These devices monitor heart rate, blood pressure, and other critical metrics, alerting users and doctors to any concerning changes. This constant vigilance allows for early detection of potential health issues, facilitating timely intervention. Additionally, AI chatbots offer 24/7 patient support, answering questions and providing medical advice. These virtual assistants enhance patient engagement, offering guidance and reassurance when in-person consultations are not possible. By bridging the gap between patients and providers, AI-powered telemedicine ensures that healthcare remains accessible and responsive, regardless of geographical barriers.

Interactive Element: Reflect on AI in Healthcare

Consider how AI might impact your own healthcare experience. Reflect on a recent medical appointment or procedure. How could AI have enhanced the diagnosis or treatment? Write down your thoughts and imagine future scenarios where AI might play a crucial role in your healthcare journey. This exercise can help you appreciate the potential of AI to transform medical care and improve personal health outcomes.

4.2 Drones and AI: Revolutionizing Aerial Technology

Today's drones can effortlessly glide over expansive fields, equipped with advanced sensors that continuously scan the terrain below. They leverage sophisticated algorithms to make instant decisions, allowing them to navigate obstacles and optimize their flight paths in real time, ensuring efficiency and safety during their missions. This image captures the essence of AI-enhanced navigation systems, a technology that has transformed drone operations. Drones equipped with AI can detect obstacles in their path, such as trees or buildings, enabling them to avoid collisions with remarkable precision. This capability relies on sophisticated algorithms that process data from sensors, allowing drones to make split-second adjustments and ensure safe navigation. These autonomous flight path optimization algorithms enhance efficiency, enabling drones to carry out complex missions without human intervention, whether inspecting infrastructure or delivering packages.

In the realm of agriculture and environmental monitoring, AI-driven drones have become invaluable tools. Imagine a farmer using a drone to survey crops, gathering data that informs decisions on irrigation and fertilization. AI-powered crop monitoring allows drones to analyze plant health, detect disease, and assess soil conditions, providing insights that enhance precision agriculture. These drones can cover large areas quickly, offering a level of detail and accuracy that traditional methods cannot match. Similarly, in environmental monitoring, drones equipped with sensors conduct surveys, collecting data on air quality, wildlife populations, and deforestation. This information is crucial for conservation efforts, enabling scientists to monitor ecosystems and respond to changes in real-time.

During disasters, the role of drones becomes even more critical, like in a natural disaster zone, where traditional access is hampered by debris and chaos. Here, AI enhances response efforts by enabling drones to map and assess affected areas swiftly and accurately. These drones provide real-time data on the extent of damage, helping emergency responders prioritize their actions. Moreover, autonomous drones deliver medical supplies to isolated areas, overcoming logistical challenges that ground vehicles cannot. This capability is especially vital in remote or inaccessible regions, where time is of the essence, and immediate aid can save lives. The ability of AI-powered drones to operate independently ensures that critical supplies reach those in need efficiently and safely.

As drones become more integrated into various sectors, regulatory and ethical considerations come to the forefront. The use of drones raises privacy concerns, particularly in sectors like surveillance and data collection. Ensuring that drones operate within legal and ethical boundaries is essential, and this involves establishing clear regulatory frameworks. These frameworks dictate where and how drones can operate, safeguarding individuals' privacy while enabling innovation. Additionally, the collection and storage of data by drones must comply with privacy laws to prevent misuse. Balancing the benefits of drone technology with these concerns requires careful oversight and ongoing dialogue between stakeholders, ensuring that drones contribute positively to society without infringing on rights.

Incorporating AI into drone technology presents challenges and opportunities, transforming industries and redefining what is possible. The ability to navigate autonomously, gather and analyze data, and respond to emergencies positions drones as powerful tools in the modern world. As they continue to evolve, the focus on ethical use and regulatory compliance will play a crucial role in their success and acceptance.

4.3 Robotics: AI-Powered Machines in Action

In some of today's factories, AI-powered robots work alongside humans, each performing tasks with precision and efficiency. This illustrates the transformative role of AI in industrial robotics, especially in manufacturing settings. Here, AI predicts when machines might fail, a practice known as predictive maintenance. By analyzing data from sensors, AI can foresee potential breakdowns, allowing for timely interventions that prevent costly downtimes. This proactive approach ensures smooth operations and extends the lifespan of machinery. Moreover, collaborative robots, or cobots, have emerged as invaluable partners to human workers. These cobots are designed to handle repetitive or dangerous tasks, freeing up human workers to focus on more complex activities. With sensors and intelligent systems, cobots adapt to their environment, ensuring safety and efficiency in shared workspaces. This synergy between humans and robots enhances productivity and creates a more dynamic work environment.

In service industries, AI robots are making a notable impact. Picture a hotel lobby where an AI robot greets guests, checks them in, and assists with inquiries. These robots, prevalent in retail and hospitality sectors, elevate customer service by delivering consistent and efficient interactions. They can handle routine tasks such as processing transactions or providing information, allowing human staff to concentrate on more personalized customer interactions. Similarly, automated cleaning and sanitation robots have become crucial in healthcare, particularly in maintaining hygiene standards. These robots efficiently clean large areas, reducing the risk of infection and ensuring a safe environment for patients and healthcare workers. Equipped with AI, they navigate hospital corridors autonomously, adapting to changes and avoiding obstacles, demonstrating the versatility and reliability of AI in service applications.

In medical environments, AI robotics have revolutionized healthcare assistance. For example, a robotic surgical assistant in an operating room, precisely guiding a surgeon's hand during a delicate procedure. These robots enhance surgical precision, reducing the likelihood of errors and improving patient outcomes. They are equipped with advanced sensors and imaging technologies, providing real-time feedback that helps surgeons make informed decisions. Beyond surgery, AI-powered exoskeletons are aiding rehabilitation, offering support to patients recovering from injuries. These wearable devices use AI to adapt to a patient's movements, providing the necessary force to assist in walking or standing. This support not only accelerates recovery but also empowers patients to regain independence, highlighting the profound impact of robotics in healthcare.

As robots become more integrated into our lives, ethical and safety considerations come to the forefront. Ensuring safety in human-robot interactions is paramount. Robots are equipped with sensors to detect human presence, allowing them to operate safely alongside people without causing harm. Moreover, addressing job displacement concerns is crucial as automation becomes more prevalent. While robots take over repetitive tasks, they also create opportunities for upskilling and new roles focused on managing and maintaining these technologies. It's essential to balance technological advancement with the human element, ensuring that societal benefits are maximized without compromising human dignity or employment. This balance is achieved through thoughtful design, robust safety protocols, and continuous dialogue between technology developers and society.

4.4 Autonomous Vehicles: The Future of Self-Driving Cars

Autonomous vehicles are designed to navigate and drive on roads without human intervention. These vehicles use various technologies, including sensors, cameras, and algorithms, to understand their environment and make real-time decisions. The development of autonomous vehicles aims to enhance road safety, reduce traffic congestion, and improve mobility. AI plays a crucial role in processing data from the vehicle's surroundings, allowing for efficient navigation through complex urban environments. At the heart of these vehicles are advanced AI technologies that enable them to perceive and navigate their surroundings with precision. Computer vision systems are crucial here, acting as the vehicle's eyes. They process real-time visual data from cameras and sensors, allowing the car to understand its environment. These systems detect road signs, lane markings, and obstacles, ensuring the vehicle can make informed navigation decisions. Alongside computer vision, machine learning algorithms are the brains behind decision-making processes. They analyze vast amounts of data, learning how to react to various driving conditions. From merging into traffic to navigating complex intersections, these algorithms enable autonomous vehicles to handle diverse scenarios safely.

The potential of AI to enhance road safety and efficiency is immense. Self-driving cars equipped with AI can react faster than human drivers, reducing the risk of accidents. For instance, AI systems can predict and avoid collisions by analyzing the behavior of surrounding vehicles and pedestrians. In emergency situations, such as sudden braking by the car in front, the AI can respond instantaneously, minimizing impact. Moreover, AI-controlled vehicles optimize traffic flow by communicating with each other and traffic management systems. This coordination reduces congestion, leading to smoother traffic movement and shorter travel times. Imagine a city where traffic lights and vehicles work in harmony, reducing gridlock and pollution. Such efficiency improvements not only enhance the driving experience but also contribute to environmental sustainability by lowering emissions.

Despite these advancements, autonomous vehicles face significant challenges and limitations. Navigating complex urban environments remains a formidable task. Cities are dynamic, with unpredictable pedestrian movements, construction zones, and varying weather conditions. AI systems must continuously learn and adapt to these complexities, ensuring safe operation. Ethical dilemmas also arise in decision-making processes. Consider a scenario where a collision is unavoidable: should the car prioritize the safety of its passengers or pedestrians? These ethical questions require careful consideration and the development of guidelines to ensure responsible AI behavior. Additionally, there are technical challenges, such as ensuring robust connectivity and cybersecurity to protect vehicles from hacking.

The path to full deployment of autonomous vehicles also involves navigating regulatory and infrastructure hurdles. Legal frameworks must address liability and accountability in the event of accidents involving self-driving cars. Determining responsibility is complex, involving manufacturers, software developers, and vehicle owners. Clear regulations are needed to establish who is accountable when things go wrong. Infrastructure modifications are equally crucial. Roads need to be equipped with sensors and communication devices to support autonomous systems. This includes smart traffic signals and dedicated lanes for autonomous vehicles. These changes require significant investment and collaboration between public and private sectors. Moreover, public acceptance plays a critical role in the widespread adoption of autonomous vehicles. Building trust in AI technology and addressing concerns about safety and privacy are essential steps in gaining consumer confidence.

4.5 AI in Climate Innovations: Tackling Environmental Challenges

In today's world, predicting climate change impacts is becoming increasingly precise; AI is playing a crucial role in revolutionizing climate modeling and prediction by enabling more accurate assessments of environmental changes and their potential consequences. This technological advancement allows for better preparedness and response strategies to address the challenges posed by climate change. With AI, scientists can now analyze vast datasets, which was once a daunting task. These models process complex environmental data, identifying patterns and trends that help predict future climate scenarios. By sifting through these datasets, AI provides insights into how our planet's climate is changing, guiding policymakers in making informed decisions about environmental protection. These predictions are crucial in understanding potential climate impacts, enabling societies to prepare for changes in weather patterns, sea levels, and biodiversity. By transforming raw data into actionable insights, AI empowers communities to anticipate and mitigate the effects of climate change, fostering resilience and sustainability.

In the realm of agriculture, AI is a game-changer, promoting sustainable farming practices that enhance productivity while conserving resources. AI technologies are transforming agriculture through precise management of various farming practices. These systems analyze soil moisture, weather forecasts, and plant health data to determine optimal water usage, ensuring that crops receive just the right amount of water. Meanwhile, AI-driven pest control identifies potential threats early, deploying targeted interventions that minimize chemical use. This precision agriculture not only boosts crop yields but also reduces waste and environmental impact. By optimizing resource use, farmers can cultivate healthier crops with fewer inputs, supporting sustainable food production that meets the demands of a growing global population.

The field of renewable energy management also benefits from AI's transformative capabilities. Solar panels and wind turbines increasingly utilize AI technology for predictive maintenance. These systems continuously monitor equipment performance, analyzing data to identify potential issues before they lead to failures. By leveraging machine learning algorithms, they can predict maintenance needs, reduce downtime, and enhance the efficiency of renewable energy generation. By analyzing data from sensors, AI predicts when maintenance is needed, preventing costly breakdowns and ensuring continuous energy generation. Additionally, AI enhances smart grid management by optimizing energy distribution. It balances supply and demand in real time, reducing energy waste and stabilizing the grid. This efficiency not only lowers costs, but also supports the integration of renewable energy sources, paving the way for a cleaner, more sustainable energy future. Through these innovations, AI accelerates the transition to renewable energy, driving progress toward a low-carbon economy.

AI's contributions extend to environmental conservation, where it plays a pivotal role in monitoring and protecting biodiversity. AI systems can now track endangered species and analyze data from remote cameras and sensors to monitor animal populations. These systems detect changes in habitats, alerting conservationists to potential threats like poaching or habitat loss. By providing real-time insights, AI enables proactive conservation efforts that protect vulnerable species. In addition, AI analyzes satellite data to study deforestation patterns, offering a comprehensive view of land use changes. This analysis informs reforestation initiatives and policy decisions, supporting efforts to combat deforestation and restore ecosystems. Through its ability to process vast amounts of data, AI enhances our understanding of complex ecosystems, guiding conservation strategies that preserve our planet's natural heritage.

As AI continues to evolve, its potential to address environmental challenges grows, offering innovative solutions that promote sustainability and resilience. The integration of AI into climate science, agriculture, energy, and conservation highlights its versatility and impact, transforming how we interact with and protect our natural world.

4.6 AI in Education: Personalized Learning Experiences

Adaptive learning platforms utilize artificial intelligence to customize educational experiences based on individual student needs. These systems collect data on a student's performance, identify strengths and weaknesses, and adjust the curriculum accordingly to optimize learning. This approach aims to enhance engagement and improve knowledge retention by providing personalized learning pathways that cater to each student's pace and preferences. These platforms employ AI-driven assessment tools that analyze students' performance in real-time. By identifying areas where a student excels or struggles, these tools customize the curriculum to fit individual needs. For instance, a student who grasps algebra quickly can be challenged with advanced problems, while another who finds it difficult can receive additional exercises and resources for better understanding. This personalized approach ensures no student is left behind, fostering an environment where everyone can thrive.

AI tutors and educational assistants further enhance learning by providing one-on-one support without time or location constraints. Virtual AI tutors can simulate personalized tutoring sessions, offering explanations and guidance similar to a human tutor but with the advantage of being available 24/7. Imagine a student tackling a complex math problem late at night, able to receive immediate help from an AI tutor. Additionally, AI chatbots equipped to answer student queries in real time can address questions as they arise, providing instant feedback and clarifications. This continuous support helps maintain student engagement and motivation, contributing to a more effective learning experience.

Beyond the classroom, AI significantly impacts educational administration, streamlining tasks that once required extensive manual effort. Automating administrative processes like grading and attendance allows educators to focus more on teaching and less on paperwork. AI systems can grade assignments with consistency and accuracy, providing detailed feedback that helps students improve. Similarly, AI analytics streamline admissions processes by analyzing applicant data efficiently, ensuring a fair and comprehensive review. This automation not only saves time but also enhances the overall efficiency of educational institutions, allowing them to allocate resources where they are most needed.

However, integrating AI into education is not without its challenges and ethical considerations. Ensuring data privacy for student information is paramount, as these systems collect and analyze vast amounts of sensitive data. Robust security measures and transparent privacy policies are essential to protect student information from unauthorized access. Additionally, addressing biases in AI educational tools is crucial to ensure fairness and inclusivity. AI systems must be designed to cater to diverse student populations, avoiding the perpetuation of existing disparities. Continuous evaluation and refinement of these technologies help mitigate biases, ensuring they support equitable learning opportunities for all students.

As we conclude this chapter on AI in specialized fields, it's clear that AI is not just a tool for automation or efficiency; it's a catalyst for innovation and transformation across various sectors. Whether enhancing healthcare, driving educational advancements, or contributing to environmental sustainability, AI's potential is vast and varied. As we move forward, the next chapter will explore how these advancements influence our daily lives, shaping the way we interact with the world and each other.

Make a Difference with Your Review

Unlock the Power of Generosity

Did you know that sharing your thoughts can make a big difference in someone else's life?

Imagine someone just like you—curious about AI but unsure where to begin. Your review of *AI for Beginners: Master AI Learning With Easy-to-Understand Tool Selection, Hands-On Practice, and Career Optimization Insights* could be the encouragement they need to start their journey.

My mission is to make learning AI simple, fun, and accessible to everyone. But I can't do it alone. Most people decide what to read based on reviews, and that's where you come in!

It costs nothing, takes less than a minute, and yet it could inspire someone to:

- Start a new career in AI.
- Learn the tools to build something amazing.
- Gain confidence in their ability to use technology.
- Transform their future with the power of AI.

By leaving a review, you help someone else discover the joys and possibilities of AI. It's an easy way to make a big difference in someone's life—whether they're a small business owner, a curious student, or a dreamer looking for a new path.

To share your thoughts and inspire others, simply scan the QR code or click the link below. Note that this link leads you to Amazon.com; if you have purchased the book outside the US, please leave a review from your home country app as you may not be able to leave reviews on the US store!

Click here to leave your review on Amazon.com

If you love helping others, you're my kind of person. Thank you for being generous with your time and your words. Your support means the world to me!

Warmly,

Eden Wilder

5

Ethics and the Human Element in AI

5.1 Understanding AI Ethics: What Beginners Need to Know

Imagine a world where machines make crucial decisions without human intervention. Picture an autonomous vehicle making split-second choices in a traffic accident or AI systems deciding who qualifies for a loan. With such power, the ethical implications of AI become critically important. The rapid integration of AI into our lives brings both opportunities and challenges, especially regarding ethics. Fundamentally, AI ethics ensure that these technologies operate within a framework of fairness, accountability, and transparency. These principles guide the development and deployment of AI, ensuring that it aligns with human values and protects individual rights. They demand that AI systems are not only effective but also equitable and explainable.

Ethical dilemmas in AI often arise in scenarios where technology intersects with human safety and privacy. Consider autonomous vehicles: these marvels of modern technology must make real-time decisions, often in life-and-death situations. In an accident, an AI must decide whose safety to prioritize, posing profound ethical questions about the value of human lives. Similarly, AI used in surveillance raises privacy concerns. While it can enhance security, it risks infringing on personal freedoms if misused or left unchecked. These dilemmas highlight the need for robust ethical guidelines that navigate the complexities of AI decision-making, balancing technological potential with moral responsibility.

Balancing innovation with responsibility is crucial in AI development. While the drive to innovate fuels progress, it must not overshadow the ethical considerations safeguarding humanity. The importance of moral guidelines in AI research cannot be overstated. They provide the framework for AI to be developed responsibly, minimizing risks while maximizing benefits. Case studies of ethical breaches, such as biased algorithms in hiring or facial recognition, underscore the consequences of neglecting ethics in AI. These examples serve as reminders of what can go wrong when ethical oversight is lacking, reinforcing the need for vigilance and integrity in AI development.

Frameworks and ethical AI guidelines are essential in steering AI development towards positive outcomes. The Organization for Economic Cooperation and Development (OECD)'s AI Principles, for instance, advocate for an AI that is transparent, accountable, and respects human rights. They emphasize the need for AI systems to be robust, secure, and safe throughout their lifecycle. Such frameworks guide policymakers and developers in creating AI systems that are trustworthy and beneficial. The Institute of Electrical and Electronics Engineers (IEEE)'s Ethically Aligned Design and the European Commission's Ethics Guidelines for Trustworthy AI also set standards for ethical AI, promoting practices that protect individual and societal values. These guidelines encourage international collaboration, fostering a global approach to ethical AI governance.

Reflection Exercise: Evaluating Ethical AI

- Reflect on a recent AI technology or application we previously discussed. Consider its potential benefits and ethical implications.

- Does this AI system uphold or challenge the principles of fairness, accountability and transparency for everyone?

- Now, reflect on how this ethical evaluation affects your perception of AI. Does it change your willingness to engage with AI technologies? Why or why not?

As AI continues to evolve, understanding its ethical dimensions becomes increasingly important. These technologies hold immense potential to transform society, but with that power comes the responsibility to ensure they are used ethically and equitably. By engaging with the ethical questions surrounding AI, you contribute to the development of technologies that enhance rather than harm our shared future.

5.2 AI and Privacy: Protecting Personal Data

In an era where every click, scroll, and swipe can be tracked, the importance of data privacy cannot be overstated. As AI systems become more sophisticated, they gather and analyze vast amounts of personal data, raising significant privacy concerns. The risks of data breaches and unauthorized access are ever-present, threatening to expose sensitive information to malicious actors. Beyond the immediate threat of identity theft or financial loss, data misuse can have profound implications for individual privacy. Your personal data, when mishandled, can lead to unwanted surveillance or profiling, affecting everything from your credit score to job prospects. This erosion of privacy extends beyond personal impact, affecting societal norms and expectations around confidentiality and consent. In a world where data is currency, protecting it becomes a fundamental right, demanding vigilant measures and robust safeguards to ensure it remains secure and private.

AI plays a pivotal role in data collection and analysis, often operating in ways that users may not fully understand. Social media platforms, for example, leverage AI to analyze user behavior, tailoring content and advertisements to individual preferences. This data-driven approach enhances user experience but also raises concerns about how much information is being collected and how it is used. AI-driven algorithms track everything from your online shopping habits to your news consumption patterns, creating detailed profiles that can be used to predict and influence your choices. While these insights offer commercial benefits, they also pose risks, as the boundaries between beneficial personalization and invasive monitoring blur. The challenge lies in striking a balance where AI enhances user experience without compromising privacy, requiring transparency and consent at every stage of data handling. Users have a right to know what data is collected, how it will be used, and the potential consequences of its exposure.

To safeguard personal data in an AI-driven world, several strategies and best practices are essential. Encryption and anonymization techniques are at the forefront of protecting data, ensuring that sensitive information remains secure even if intercepted. Encryption transforms data into a code, unreadable without a specific key, while anonymization removes or modifies personal identifiers, making data less traceable to individuals. These methods are vital for maintaining confidentiality, especially in industries handling large volumes of sensitive data, such as healthcare or finance. Transparency in AI data policies is equally important. Organizations must clearly communicate their data practices, allowing users to make informed decisions about their privacy. This transparency builds trust, encouraging users to confidently engage with AI technologies. Moreover, regular audits and assessments of data management practices help identify vulnerabilities and ensure compliance with privacy standards, fostering a culture of continuous improvement and accountability.

Legal and regulatory frameworks are crucial in protecting data privacy and establishing guidelines and obligations for organizations handling personal data. The General Data Protection Regulation (GDPR) in the European Union sets a high standard for data protection, granting individuals greater control over their data. It enforces strict rules on data handling and imposes significant penalties for non-compliance, encouraging organizations to prioritize privacy in their operations. Similarly, the California Consumer Privacy Act (CCPA) enhances privacy rights for residents of California, requiring businesses to disclose data collection practices and allowing consumers to opt out of data sales. These regulations reflect a growing recognition of data privacy as a fundamental right, pushing organizations to adopt responsible data practices. As AI continues to evolve, these frameworks will need to adapt, addressing new challenges and ensuring privacy protections keep pace with technological advancements.

Amidst these complexities, the responsibility of data protection extends beyond legal compliance. It requires a commitment to ethical data stewardship, where organizations prioritize user privacy and uphold the trust placed in them. As individuals, understanding your rights and the tools available to protect your data empowers you to engage with AI technologies safely and responsibly. By embracing privacy-enhancing practices and demanding transparency, you contribute to a digital ecosystem that respects and protects individual privacy, ensuring that AI serves as a force for good in society.

5.3 The Human Touch: Why AI Will Not Replace All Jobs

AI's potential to complement human labor is vast, offering new dimensions to how we work. Rather than replacing humans, AI often augments decision-making processes, enhancing our capabilities. For instance, in data analysis, AI can sift through massive datasets, identifying patterns and insights that might take a person considerable time to discover. This allows professionals to focus on strategic thinking and creative problem-solving, leveraging AI's analytical power to inform their decisions. In collaborative settings, AI serves as a partner rather than a replacement. Consider customer service roles where AI chatbots handle routine inquiries, freeing human agents to tackle more complex issues that require empathy and nuanced understanding. This collaboration ensures efficiency without sacrificing the human element essential for quality customer interactions.

As AI continues to evolve, it reshapes job roles, creating new opportunities and redefining existing ones. The rise of AI oversight and maintenance roles exemplifies this shift. These positions involve monitoring AI systems, ensuring they function correctly and ethically. Additionally, new professions have emerged, such as AI trainers who teach systems to understand specific contexts better and AI ethicists who guide the ethical development of technologies. These roles demonstrate how AI's integration into the workforce spurs innovation, prompting the creation of jobs that didn't exist a decade ago. Across sectors like healthcare, finance, and creative industries, AI-related professions are opening doors to those willing to adapt and learn. This evolution in the job market highlights AI's role as a catalyst for growth and change rather than a threat to employment.

The dynamic landscape of AI-driven work underscores the importance of skill development and lifelong learning. As AI technologies advance, so must our skills and competencies. Upskilling and reskilling initiatives are crucial, offering workers the tools to remain relevant in their fields. These programs can range from technical training in AI and data analytics to developing soft skills like critical thinking and adaptability. Educational institutions also play a pivotal role in preparing future workers, integrating AI literacy into curricula and fostering an understanding of its applications and implications. By equipping students with the knowledge to navigate AI's complexities, we prepare a workforce ready to thrive in a tech-driven world. Emphasizing continuous learning ensures that individuals can pivot as needed, embracing new opportunities that AI presents.

Examples of successful AI-human collaboration in the workplace are abundant, illustrating the synergy between technology and human creativity. In creative industries, AI enhances artistic output by offering tools that expand creative possibilities. Musicians use AI to compose new melodies, exploring combinations that inspire unique compositions. Visual artists employ AI to generate designs that merge traditional techniques with digital innovation. These collaborations allow artists to push boundaries, blending human intuition with machine precision. In healthcare, professionals harness AI for improved diagnostics, using algorithms to detect diseases with greater accuracy and speed. Radiologists, for instance, work alongside AI systems that highlight anomalies in scans, streamlining the diagnostic process and enabling earlier intervention. This partnership empowers healthcare providers to offer more effective care, combining AI's data processing prowess with human empathy and expertise.

5.4 Bias in AI: Recognizing and Mitigating It

Understanding bias in artificial intelligence is critical because it highlights the limitations and challenges of these systems. AI bias emerges when algorithms reflect the prejudices in the data they are trained on. This can skew decision-making processes, leading to unfair or inaccurate outcomes. For instance, if a machine learning model is trained on data that predominantly features one demographic, it might perform poorly when applied to a broader population. This inadequacy becomes evident in AI systems that make decisions about credit scores, hiring, or even law enforcement, where biased outcomes can have serious consequences. Bias in AI doesn't just affect individual outcomes; it can reinforce societal inequities, making it a significant issue to address.

Identifying the sources of bias in AI involves examining both the data and the algorithms themselves. Historical data biases often seep into AI predictions, creating a feedback loop perpetuating existing inequalities. For example, if historical data shows a pattern of hiring predominantly white male candidates for tech roles, an AI system trained on this data might unfairly favor white male applicants, assuming they are more qualified. Algorithmic bias can also arise from the models used to process language. AI language models might generate biased text because they reflect societal stereotypes present in the data they were trained on. These biases can manifest in subtle ways, such as favoring particular dialects or using gendered language, which can influence how users perceive the AI and its recommendations.

To mitigate bias in AI systems, diverse and representative datasets are crucial. By ensuring that training data includes a wide range of demographics, AI developers can create models that better reflect society's diversity. This diversity in data helps AI systems make more accurate and equitable decisions. Regular audits and testing for bias in AI tools also play a vital role. These audits involve evaluating the AI's performance across different groups and scenarios, identifying where biases might exist, and adjusting algorithms accordingly. By continuously testing and refining AI systems, developers can reduce prejudice and improve fairness, leading to more trustworthy and reliable outcomes.

Real-world examples illustrate the significant consequences of bias in AI. In facial recognition technology, racial bias has resulted in systems that are less accurate for people with darker skin tones. This discrepancy stems from training datasets that underrepresent diverse skin tones, leading to errors in identification and potential misuse. Similarly, gender bias in hiring algorithms has been documented, where systems trained on historical hiring data tend to favor male candidates. These biases often arise from the underrepresentation of women in certain fields or the presence of gendered language in job descriptions. Such examples underscore the importance of addressing bias in AI, as the repercussions can affect employment opportunities, civil liberties, and even personal safety.

> *Case Study: Addressing Bias in Facial Recognition*
> *Facial recognition technology has faced scrutiny due to its propensity for racial bias. A notable example is its use in law enforcement, where inaccuracies can lead to wrongful accusations and arrests. The technology often misidentifies individuals with darker skin tones due to biased training data, which predominantly features lighter-skinned individuals. To address this, developers are working to create more diverse datasets and improve algorithmic accuracy. Organizations like the Algorithmic Justice League advocate for transparency and fairness in AI systems, promoting awareness and accountability. Through these efforts, the goal is to develop facial recognition technology that is both effective and equitable.*

Recognizing and mitigating bias in AI is a complex but necessary task. By understanding its sources, implementing diverse datasets, and conducting regular audits, we can work towards AI systems that serve everyone fairly and justly. These efforts not only improve the technology but also ensure that AI's impact on society is positive and inclusive.

5.5 The Societal Impact of AI: Opportunities and Challenges

As we've seen in the previous chapters, AI has transformed healthcare and education, making them more efficient and accessible. In healthcare, AI's potential is immense. It assists doctors by predicting patient outcomes, analyzing medical images, and suggesting treatment plans. This not only speeds up diagnosis but also improves accuracy, potentially saving lives. AI also plays a crucial role in managing healthcare logistics, optimizing resources, and ensuring that patients receive timely care. In education, AI personalizes learning experiences, adapting to individual student needs. This approach helps educators identify areas where students struggle and tailor lessons accordingly, enhancing both engagement and understanding. Moreover, AI-driven tools break down language barriers, providing multilingual support and opening doors for students previously sidelined due to language constraints. Beyond these core areas, AI also enhances accessibility for individuals with disabilities. Voice-activated assistants help those with mobility challenges, while text-to-speech and speech-to-text technologies empower individuals with visual and auditory impairments. These applications demonstrate AI's potential to create a more inclusive society where technology bridges gaps and offers equal opportunities for all.

Despite its benefits, AI integration poses challenges that must be addressed. The digital divide remains a significant barrier, with unequal access to AI technologies widening the gap between different socioeconomic groups. While some enjoy the latest advancements, others lack the infrastructure or resources to benefit from AI, exacerbating existing inequalities. This divide impacts education, employment, and access to essential services, highlighting the need for policies that promote equitable AI access. Ethical concerns also loom large, particularly regarding AI surveillance and control. The potential for AI to infringe on privacy and civil liberties is a growing worry. As AI systems become more pervasive, the risk of misuse or overreach increases, raising questions about who controls these technologies and how they are governed. These challenges underscore the need for robust ethical frameworks and transparent governance to ensure that AI serves humanity positively.

Public perception plays a crucial role in AI adoption and trust. Many people are wary of AI, fearing its potential to operate autonomously and without accountability. Building trust requires transparency in AI operations, where users understand how AI systems work and the data they use. This transparency fosters confidence, allowing people to engage with AI technologies without fear. Addressing fears of AI autonomy and control is also essential. While AI can operate independently, ensuring that human oversight remains a priority is crucial. This balance reassures the public that AI will not operate unchecked, safeguarding against unintended consequences. Clear communication about AI's capabilities and limitations helps demystify the technology, promoting a more informed and accepting society.

Case studies reveal AI's societal impact, illustrating its promise and pitfalls. In disaster management, AI enhances response efforts by predicting natural disasters and coordinating relief operations. AI systems analyze data from various sources, providing real-time insights that aid in decision-making and resource allocation. This capability improves the speed and efficiency of emergency responses, potentially saving lives and reducing damage. However, AI-driven public surveillance systems raise privacy concerns. While they can enhance security, they also risk infringing on individual freedoms if not properly regulated. These systems often collect vast amounts of data, leading to potential misuse or unauthorized access. Balancing the benefits of AI surveillance with privacy rights is a delicate task, requiring careful consideration to prevent abuse. These examples underscore AI's dual nature, where its potential for good must be weighed against the risks it poses. As AI continues to evolve, understanding its societal impact remains paramount, guiding its development in ways that align with shared values and goals.

5.6 AI and Cultural Sensitivity: Global Perspectives

AI's influence on cultural norms and practices is profound, shaping how we communicate, create, and preserve our heritage. Language preservation is one area where AI's impact is particularly noticeable. In a world with thousands of languages, many of which are at risk of extinction, AI offers tools for documentation and learning. Machine translation and language processing technologies enable the preservation of indigenous languages, making them accessible to future generations. For instance, with Google Translate, you can converse with someone in your own language, and the app will translate it into the other person's language. These tools also facilitate cross-cultural communication, breaking down language barriers and fostering global understanding. Moreover, AI plays a role in cultural content creation and curation. Artists and curators use AI to generate new works and organize existing collections, exploring cultural themes in innovative ways. AI can analyze vast archives, uncovering patterns and connections that might otherwise remain hidden, enriching our understanding of cultural histories and narratives.

Incorporating cultural sensitivity in AI development is crucial to ensuring that these technologies respect diverse traditions and values. One important aspect is ensuring cultural representation in AI datasets. When datasets reflect the diversity of human experiences, AI systems can better understand and respond to different cultural contexts. This diversity helps avoid cultural stereotypes in AI-generated content, which can perpetuate biases and misunderstandings. Developers must be mindful of the cultural nuances embedded in language, imagery, and behavior, creating AI that resonates authentically with various communities. By prioritizing cultural sensitivity, AI can become a tool for inclusion and celebration rather than homogenizing global diversity.

AI applications adapted to diverse cultural settings illustrate the technology's versatility and potential for positive impact. In developing countries, AI addresses local challenges by providing solutions tailored to specific needs. For example, AI-driven agricultural tools offer farmers in rural areas insights into crop management, improving yield and sustainability. These tools consider local environmental conditions and cultural practices, offering tailored advice that traditional systems might overlook. Similarly, culturally tailored AI educational tools enhance learning experiences by aligning with students' cultural backgrounds. By integrating local history, language, and customs into educational content, AI makes learning more relevant and engaging, fostering a sense of identity and pride.

However, achieving cultural sensitivity in AI is not without challenges. Balancing globalization with cultural preservation requires careful consideration. While AI promotes global connectivity, it also risks overshadowing local traditions and languages, leading to cultural homogenization. Addressing linguistic diversity in AI applications is another challenge, as many languages still need to be represented in datasets. This lack of representation can limit AI's ability to serve all communities equitably. Ensuring that AI respects cultural differences involves ongoing dialogue and collaboration with diverse stakeholders, including cultural experts, linguists, and community leaders. By engaging with these voices, developers can create AI systems that honor and uplift cultural heritage.

As we navigate the complexities of AI and cultural sensitivity, it's clear that technology is both a bridge and a barrier. It has the power to connect us, yet also the potential to divide. By understanding and respecting cultural differences, we can harness AI's potential to enrich our collective human experience, ensuring that it reflects the diverse tapestry of our world.

6

Overcoming Common Obstacles in AI Learning

6.1 Fear of Mistakes: Turning Errors into Learning Experiences

When you start learning about AI, you may encounter new concepts and techniques that are unfamiliar. The journey can involve various topics, including machine learning, neural networks, and data processing. The path of learning AI requires patience and persistence, as the field is constantly evolving and advancing. The world of artificial intelligence is vast and complex, often leaving beginners feeling overwhelmed and hesitant to make mistakes. Yet, just like discovering a new path, embracing these uncertainties can lead to amazing opportunities for growth and innovation. It's not about avoiding errors but learning from them and seeing each misstep as a valuable lesson. This mindset is crucial in AI, where trial and error are part of the journey to understanding and mastery.

Embracing errors as learning opportunities is not just a comforting thought but a practical approach endorsed by many AI pioneers. Andrew Ng, a prominent figure in AI, often emphasizes the importance of iteration and learning from failure. The process of refining algorithms and models through trial and error is where true innovation happens. Consider a well-known case study of an AI project focused on developing a speech recognition system. The initial models were flawed, struggling with accuracy and noise interference. However, by analyzing these errors and iterating on the design, the developers were able to improve the system significantly. Each failure provided insights that guided the next steps, turning setbacks into stepping stones. The result was a more robust and effective tool that exceeded initial expectations.

Common mistakes in AI learning are part of the process, and recognizing them is the first step toward avoiding them. Overfitting is a frequent pitfall beginners encounter. This occurs when a model learns the training data too well, capturing noise and random fluctuations rather than the underlying pattern. The model performs well on training data but poorly on new data. To avoid this, you can use techniques such as cross-validation and regularization, which help the model generalize unseen data better. Another common issue is misinterpreting AI predictions due to a lack of context. AI models provide outputs based on patterns they recognize, but without context, these predictions can be misleading. It's essential to combine AI insights with human judgment, ensuring that decisions are well-informed and accurate.

Building resilience and confidence in AI learning involves setting realistic goals and celebrating small victories along the way. Start by setting achievable milestones that break down complex tasks into manageable steps. This approach keeps you motivated and focused, as each milestone reached is a testament to your progress. Celebrate these small successes, whether it's successfully implementing a new algorithm or debugging a tricky issue. Acknowledging these achievements boosts confidence and prepares you for tackling more challenging problems. Remember that AI learning is a marathon, not a sprint. It requires patience, persistence, and a willingness to embrace challenges as opportunities for growth.

Interactive Element: Reflect and Learn

Think about a recent mistake you made while learning AI. Reflect on what went wrong, what you learned, and how you can apply this knowledge in the future. Write down your thoughts in a journal, creating a personal record of your learning journey. This exercise helps solidify your understanding and reminds you that mistakes are part of the process.

As you continue on this path, remember that overcoming obstacles in AI learning involves embracing errors, avoiding common pitfalls, and building resilience through practice and reflection. With each challenge, you gain valuable insights, turning mistakes into catalysts for growth and innovation.

6.2 Keeping Up with AI Trends: Staying Informed

AI evolves at a pace that can make your head spin. One moment, a groundbreaking model emerges; the next, it's been refined or surpassed. This rapid evolution is part of what makes AI so exciting, yet it also presents a challenge. Keeping up with the latest trends isn't just about staying informed; it's about staying relevant in a field where yesterday's knowledge can quickly become outdated. Key areas to monitor include advancements in machine learning, natural language processing, and computer vision. Each area is a hub of innovation, driven by emerging technologies like quantum computing and edge AI. These technologies are reshaping how we think about AI and expanding its potential applications across industries. Understanding these trends helps you anticipate changes and adapt your learning strategy accordingly.

Reliable sources for AI news and updates are essential in navigating this fast-paced world. Subscribing to AI-focused newsletters and journals can provide daily or weekly doses of the latest developments.

Newsletters like "Mindstream" and "The Neuron," with their substantial subscriber bases, offer insights and trends in AI, keeping you abreast of what's new and noteworthy. They distill complex topics into digestible content, making it easier to understand and apply. Following AI influencers and experts on social media platforms is another effective way to stay updated. Influencers like Andrew Ng and Fei-Fei Li share valuable insights and often highlight key advancements in the field. Their posts can provide context and clarity, guiding you through the intricacies of AI developments.

Engaging with AI communities and forums is a powerful way to enhance your knowledge and connect with like-minded individuals. Platforms like Reddit and Discord host vibrant discussions where you can ask questions, share insights, and learn from others. Subreddits such as r/OpenAI and r/MachineLearning are filled with discussions ranging from beginner topics to advanced concepts, offering a wealth of information and community support. Participating in these discussions not only broadens your understanding but also allows you to contribute your perspective. Attending AI webinars and virtual conferences is another way to engage with the community. These events provide opportunities to hear from industry leaders, learn about cutting-edge research, and network with professionals from around the world. They offer a glimpse into the future of AI, inspiring new ideas and collaborations.

Continuous learning is the cornerstone of success in AI, and setting up alerts for AI-related keywords is a practical strategy to stay informed. These alerts, whether through Google or specialized AI platforms, ensure you receive updates on relevant topics as they happen. This real-time information keeps you ahead of the curve, allowing you to explore new developments as they unfold. Enrolling in ongoing education programs and workshops is another effective way to deepen your understanding. Many universities and organizations offer courses tailored to different levels of expertise, providing structured learning paths that build on your existing knowledge. These programs often include hands-on projects and collaborations, translating theory into practice. By committing to continuous learning, you can develop a robust understanding of AI, equipping yourself with the skills and insights needed to thrive in this dynamic field.

6.3 Building a Supportive AI Learning Community

A thriving AI learning community typically resembles a busy café, where many individuals gather to collaborate and discuss various topics related to artificial intelligence. These communities often include students, professionals, and enthusiasts who share knowledge, exchange ideas, and work on projects together. They provide a supportive environment for learning through workshops, seminars, and networking opportunities, fostering growth and innovation in the field of AI. The power of community in AI learning is immense, offering a supportive environment where individuals can grow, share, and innovate together. In such a community, peer mentorship plays a pivotal role. It's about learning from one another, exchanging ideas, and supporting each other through challenges. When you collaborate with others, you gain insights that you might not have considered on your own. Sharing resources, such as tutorials, datasets, or coding scripts, enhances everyone's learning experience. It creates a network where knowledge flows freely, empowering each member to reach their full potential.

Collaborative learning through group projects further enriches this experience. Imagine working with a diverse group of people, each bringing unique skills and perspectives to the table. Together, you tackle complex problems, brainstorm solutions, and build innovative AI models. This collaborative approach not only deepens your understanding but also fosters teamwork and communication skills—attributes that are invaluable in any professional setting. By contributing to group projects, you learn to appreciate different viewpoints and develop a more holistic understanding of AI. It's this shared journey that transforms individual learning into a collective achievement, making the process more enjoyable and rewarding.

Finding and joining supportive AI communities is easier than you might think. Online platforms like LinkedIn groups and Discord channels are great places to start. These platforms host numerous AI-focused groups where enthusiasts and professionals gather to discuss trends, share resources, and provide support. Joining these communities gives you access to a wealth of knowledge and a network of like-minded individuals eager to learn and grow. Local meetups and AI clubs offer another avenue for engagement. These gatherings provide opportunities to connect in person, attend workshops, and participate in discussions. Whether you're attending a tech talk or collaborating on a project, these interactions enrich your learning experience and expand your professional network.

Contributing to the growth of AI communities involves more than just participation. It's about actively sharing your insights and experiences. Whether you're a seasoned professional or a curious beginner, your unique perspective adds value to the community. By sharing your experiences, you help others navigate similar challenges and inspire new ideas. Organizing and participating in AI workshops and hackathons is another way to contribute. These events bring together individuals with diverse skills to solve real-world problems, fostering creativity and innovation. By taking part, you not only enhance your skills but also help build a stronger, more connected community.

Supportive learning environments are not just theoretical concepts; they exist and thrive in various forms. Consider the case of an AI study group formed by students at a university. Despite having different levels of expertise, the group committed to meeting regularly to discuss AI concepts and work on projects. Over time, they collectively developed a sophisticated AI model that garnered attention and accolades. This success story illustrates the power of community learning, where shared goals and mutual support lead to remarkable achievements. Testimonials from members of thriving AI communities echo similar sentiments. They often describe their experiences as transformative, highlighting the friendships and professional connections they've made along the way.

The value of a supportive AI learning community cannot be overstated. It offers a nurturing environment where you can thrive, explore, and innovate without fear of judgment. In these communities, learning becomes a shared endeavor filled with encouragement and inspiration. Whether online or in-person, the connections you make can open doors to new opportunities, provide guidance, and offer a sense of belonging. As you navigate the world of AI, consider the impact of community and the role it can play in enhancing your learning journey. Engage, contribute, and grow with others who share your passion for AI. Together, you can achieve more than you ever thought possible.

6.4 Balancing Theory and Practice: Seamless Integration

Imagine trying to learn how to swim by reading a book about it, but never actually getting into the water. While the theory provides essential knowledge, true understanding only comes when you take the plunge and experience it firsthand. This analogy holds true in the world of AI as well. Balancing theory and practice is crucial for developing a comprehensive understanding of AI concepts. Engaging with theoretical knowledge helps you grasp the fundamental principles and frameworks that underpin AI technologies. However, without applying these concepts practically, you miss out on the nuances and complexities that can only be appreciated through experience. Integrating both elements enables you to see the bigger picture, making connections between abstract ideas and their tangible applications.

Applying theoretical knowledge in practical scenarios is where the magic happens. Take machine learning algorithms, for instance. You might study various algorithms, understanding their mechanics and mathematical foundations. But it's when you implement these algorithms on real-world datasets that things click into place. Consider a dataset containing customer reviews for a product. By applying sentiment analysis—a common machine learning task—you can categorize reviews as positive, negative, or neutral. This practical application reinforces your theoretical understanding, allowing you to see how algorithms function in real-life situations and how they can be tweaked to improve performance. Beyond sentiment analysis, building simple AI models can further solidify your learning. Creating a basic neural network to recognize handwritten digits, for instance, gives you a firsthand look at how data flows through layers and how weights and biases influence outcomes.

Developing hands-on projects is an excellent way to bridge the gap between theory and practice. These projects serve as a laboratory where you can experiment with different techniques and approaches, learning from both successes and failures. By creating a personal portfolio of AI projects, you not only document your learning journey but also showcase your skills to potential employers or collaborators. Your portfolio might include a variety of projects, from a chatbot designed to answer customer queries to a predictive model that forecasts stock prices. Each project adds to your understanding and demonstrates your ability to apply AI concepts creatively and effectively. Engaging in AI competitions and challenges is another avenue that accelerates learning. Platforms like Kaggle offer a treasure trove of datasets and problems to solve, providing a real-world context for your skills. Competing against others pushes you to innovate and refine your techniques, while the community feedback helps you grow and improve.

Evaluating and reflecting on your learning is a vital part of the process, ensuring that your efforts translate into meaningful progress. Self-assessment quizzes and practical tests can help determine where you stand and what areas need more attention. These assessments challenge you to apply what you've learned in new situations, deepening your understanding and highlighting gaps in knowledge. Keeping a learning journal is another powerful tool for reflection. By documenting your experiences, insights, and challenges, you create a record of your growth. This journal can serve as a source of motivation, reminding you of how far you've come and the obstacles you've overcome. It also helps you identify patterns in your learning, guiding you toward more effective strategies and practices.

Balancing theory and practice in AI learning is an ongoing process requiring dedication and curiosity. It's about continually exploring new concepts while applying them in practical, meaningful ways. This balance enriches your understanding, builds confidence, and prepares you for the challenges and opportunities in the AI field. As you integrate these elements into your learning journey, remember that each step brings you closer to mastering the intricacies of AI, unlocking its potential to transform ideas into reality.

7

AI for Career Enhancement and Personal Development

7.1 AI for Resume Building: Stand Out in the Job Market

Imagine you're about to refresh your resume, a document that's your gateway to new opportunities. But instead of the usual struggle, you have a secret weapon—AI tools that transform your resume into a standout masterpiece. In today's job market, where competition is fierce, having a resume that not only highlights your skills but also catches the eye of automated systems is crucial. This chapter delves into how AI can enhance your resume-building process, making it both impactful and efficient.

Creating a resume that truly reflects your capabilities is no small feat, but AI tools can simplify this task significantly. Start by exploring AI-generated templates on Camva or resume.io, which provide a polished and professional layout. These templates are designed to make your resume visually appealing while ensuring the content is easy to read. They guide you in presenting your skills and experiences in a structured manner, highlighting your AI-related competencies effectively. It's like having a seasoned designer at your fingertips, ensuring that your resume not only looks good but also communicates your qualifications clearly. By leveraging these templates, you can focus on what truly matters—showcasing the unique skills and experiences that set you apart from other candidates.

In the digital age, many companies use Applicant Tracking Systems (ATS) to filter through the influx of resumes they receive. These systems scan resumes for specific keywords, determining which candidates make it through to the next round. Optimizing your resume for ATS is vital, and AI comes in handy here. Use AI tools to identify industry-specific keywords that are relevant to the job you're applying for. These tools analyze job descriptions and suggest keywords that align with the role, ensuring your resume is tailored to pass through ATS filters successfully. Tailoring your resume for specific job descriptions not only increases your chances of getting noticed but also demonstrates your attention to detail and understanding of the role.

Including AI projects and experiences on your resume can significantly enhance its appeal. Whether you've worked on AI projects at school or as part of your job, these experiences showcase your practical skills and ability to apply AI concepts effectively. Describe your contributions in detail, focusing on the impact and outcomes of your work. If you have one, include links to online portfolios where recruiters can explore your projects further. This transparency not only highlights your technical skills but also your initiative and creativity. Demonstrating real-world applications of AI in your resume can be a game-changer, setting you apart as a candidate who can bring tangible value to the organization.

Once your resume is drafted, AI tools like Jobscan and Resume Worded can provide invaluable feedback. These tools analyze your resume for readability and impact, offering suggestions on how to enhance its effectiveness. They highlight areas where your resume might fall short and provide actionable insights for improvement. Whether it's adjusting the structure for better flow or refining the language to make it more engaging, these tools act as a second pair of eyes, helping you polish your resume to perfection. Their feedback ensures that your resume not only meets industry standards but also resonates with both human readers and ATS.

> *Interactive Element: Resume Checklist for AI Integration*
> *- Choose an AI-generated template for a clean, professional layout. Try Canva or Resume.io.*
> *- Highlight your skills and experiences prominently.*
> *- Use AI tools to identify industry-specific keywords for your domain.*
> *- Tailor your resume to match specific job descriptions.*
> *- Include detailed descriptions of projects and tasks you've done and provide portfolio links if you have them.*
> *- Use AI tools like Jobscan and Resume Worded for feedback and refinement.*

By embracing these AI tools and techniques, you can craft a resume that truly stands out, opening doors to new career opportunities and setting the stage for personal and professional growth in the ever-evolving job market.

7.2 AI for Students: Supplementing Academic Learning

Imagine you're a student working on a research project tasked with analyzing vast datasets. Here, AI becomes your ally. Tools designed for data analysis can sift through information, revealing patterns and insights that might take you hours to uncover manually. For instance, platforms like IBM's Watson Analytics offer AI-driven data exploration, making complex analysis more intuitive. These tools help you understand trends and correlations, providing a solid foundation for your research conclusions. Imagine the efficiency of having AI assist in collaborative studies, where students from different backgrounds share data and insights in real time. AI platforms facilitate this by offering seamless integration of ideas, allowing for dynamic teamwork and enriched learning experiences.

Beyond research, AI serves as a powerful learning aid, enhancing the way students acquire knowledge. Personalized learning apps, such as Duolingo for language acquisition or Khan Academy's AI-driven lessons, tailor educational content to individual learning paces and styles. These apps adapt to your progress, offering challenges that match your current level, ensuring that learning remains engaging and effective. Meanwhile, AI tools for time management, like Todoist or My Study Life, organize study schedules and deadlines, helping you balance academic commitments. By automating reminders and structuring your tasks, these tools free you to focus on what truly matters—understanding and mastering the material.

As you look toward a future career, education and internships become vital stepping stones. Selecting relevant courses and electives is crucial. Universities often offer programs that cover machine learning, data science, and AI ethics, providing a comprehensive foundation in the field. Engaging in internships further enhances this learning. These experiences allow you to apply theoretical knowledge to real-world challenges, gaining insights into the industry's dynamics and expectations. Practical experience not only solidifies your understanding but also builds a professional network, connecting you with mentors and peers who share your passions.

Highlighting academic achievements related to your field is essential in showcasing your capabilities. Presenting research findings at academic conferences demonstrates your expertise and commitment to the field. These events offer a platform to share your work, receive feedback, and engage with the community. Publishing field-related papers in student journals is another avenue to highlight your accomplishments. It allows you to contribute to the body of knowledge, sharing your insights and findings with a broader audience. These achievements not only enrich your academic profile but also enhance your resume, positioning you as a knowledgeable and proactive candidate in the AI job market.

Visual Element: Academic Presentation Checklist
- *Ensure clarity and conciseness in your presentation slides.*
- *Highlight key findings and their implications clearly.*
- *Engage your audience with visual aids like graphs and info-graphics.*
- *Practice delivery to maintain confidence and clarity.*
- *Prepare for questions by anticipating audience inquiries.*

By embracing AI tools in your academic journey, you can enhance your learning, prepare for a successful career, and effectively communicate your achievements.

7.3 AI Skills for Career Optimizers: Enhancing Current Roles

In the fast-paced world of work, integrating AI into your current job can be a game changer. Imagine you're in marketing, tasked with analyzing consumer behavior. AI tools can help you sift through vast amounts of data, uncovering trends and insights that might otherwise remain hidden. This isn't just about crunching numbers—it's about understanding your audience better, allowing you to tailor marketing strategies with precision. For instance, AI can identify which campaigns resonate most with your target demographic, helping you allocate resources more effectively. This level of insight not only boosts efficiency but also enhances the impact of your marketing efforts, ultimately driving growth.

Customer service is another area where AI can significantly enhance performance. Think of AI chatbots, which can handle routine inquiries at any hour, providing instant support to users. They free up human agents to focus on more complex issues, improving overall efficiency. These chatbots learn from interactions, becoming more effective over time, and can offer personalized responses based on previous customer interactions. This level of service enhances customer satisfaction, building loyalty and trust. By incorporating AI into customer service, you not only streamline operations but also create a more responsive and user-friendly experience.

Staying relevant in today's workforce means continuously learning and adapting. Upskilling and reskilling are crucial steps to remain competitive. Many online platforms offer courses focused on AI skills development, ranging from introductory to advanced levels. Websites like Coursera and edX provide courses led by industry experts, covering topics such as machine learning, data science, and AI ethics. Certification programs offer structured learning paths, equipping you with the credentials to back up your skills. These courses are flexible, allowing you to learn at your own pace, making it easier to balance with existing work commitments.

Demonstrating AI proficiency to your employer is essential for career advancement. Presenting AI-driven project outcomes is one way to showcase your skills. Whether it's a successful campaign analysis or an improved customer service process, highlight the tangible benefits AI brought to the project. Visual aids like charts or infographics can effectively communicate these results, making your achievements clear and impactful. Leading AI initiatives within your team also demonstrates leadership and innovation. By spearheading these projects, you position yourself as a forward-thinker within the organization, someone who embraces new technologies and drives progress.

Consider the finance sector, where AI tools have revolutionized productivity. Automated algorithms analyze financial data at lightning speed, identifying patterns and predicting market trends. This allows financial analysts to make informed decisions quickly, maximizing investment returns. Similarly, in supply chain management, AI enhances decision-making by optimizing logistics and predicting demand accurately. These improvements reduce costs and increase efficiency, providing a competitive edge. Professionals who adapt AI to their roles not only enhance their performance but also contribute significantly to their organization's success.

7.4 Career Change with AI: New Opportunities and Roles

If you're contemplating a career change or a second job to make ends meet, AI offers such a landscape, with a plethora of roles emerging across diverse sectors. Data scientists, for instance, are in high demand in industries ranging from healthcare to finance. They analyze complex datasets to extract actionable insights, driving decisions that shape future strategies. But data science isn't the only path. Consider roles like AI ethics and compliance officers, which focus on ensuring AI systems adhere to ethical guidelines and regulatory standards. These positions are crucial as AI integration grows, requiring a blend of technical knowledge and ethical foresight to navigate the complex landscape of AI governance.

Transitioning into AI doesn't mean starting from scratch. Many skills you already possess can be leveraged in this new domain. Analytical skills, for example, are invaluable in AI data analysis, where interpreting patterns and trends is key. Creative problem-solving, too, is essential in AI development, as it involves devising innovative solutions to novel challenges. These skills, honed in other fields, can seamlessly transfer to AI, enriching your new role with a unique perspective. It's about recognizing how your existing expertise aligns with AI's requirements and using that as a foundation to build upon. This approach not only eases the transition but also positions you as a versatile and adaptable candidate in the AI industry.

To successfully transition, a structured plan is essential. Start by setting clear short and long-term goals, outlining where you want to be in the next few years. Identify the skills and knowledge gaps you need to address and seek out training programs or courses that can help you fill these gaps. Platforms like Coursera and Udacity offer specialized courses that cater to different experience levels, providing flexibility and accessibility. Consider pursuing certifications in areas like machine learning or data science to bolster your credentials. This structured approach provides a roadmap, guiding your transition and ensuring you stay focused and motivated.

Real-life success stories of career transitions into AI can be both inspiring and instructive. Take, for example, professionals from traditional tech roles who have successfully pivoted to AI. By building on their existing technical skills and acquiring new AI-specific knowledge, they've carved out rewarding careers in fields like AI research and development. Similarly, individuals from non-tech backgrounds have found new opportunities in AI by leveraging their unique skills. For instance, a marketing professional with strong analytical abilities might transition into AI-driven market analysis, while a creative writer could explore roles in AI content generation. These stories highlight the diverse pathways into AI, emphasizing that with the right mindset and preparation, a career change into this dynamic field is well within reach.

7.5 Entrepreneurial Ventures: AI in Business Startups

Startups can now launch with the efficiency and speed typical of experienced businesses when leveraging the capabilities of artificial intelligence. AI acts as the catalyst for this innovation, transforming ideas into reality at a pace previously unimaginable. In the realm of product development, AI tools enable rapid prototyping, allowing entrepreneurs to test and refine concepts with unprecedented speed. By simulating various scenarios, AI helps businesses anticipate challenges and optimize solutions before products even hit the market. This capability not only saves time but also reduces costs, providing an edge over competitors still reliant on traditional methods. Meanwhile, AI-driven market analysis offers insights that guide strategic decisions. By analyzing trends and consumer behaviors, AI helps entrepreneurs identify opportunities and tailor their offerings to meet specific demands. This strategic advantage is crucial in today's fast-paced business environment, where staying ahead of the curve is key to success.

Starting an AI-based business requires a keen eye for identifying niche markets that can benefit from AI solutions. Consider industries where AI can address existing inefficiencies or create entirely new possibilities. For instance, the healthcare sector is ripe for AI innovation, with opportunities ranging from personalized medicine to predictive analytics for patient care. Once a niche is identified, the next step is to build a business model with AI at its core. This involves not only developing AI-driven products or services but also integrating AI into every aspect of the business, from operations to customer engagement. Such a model ensures that AI is not just a tool but a fundamental component driving growth and differentiation in the market.

Funding is often a major hurdle for startups, but the rise of AI has attracted a wealth of investment opportunities. Venture capitalists and angel investors specializing in AI are actively seeking innovative ideas that leverage AI's potential. These investors understand the transformative power of AI and are willing to fund ventures that demonstrate a clear vision and scalable potential. Additionally, government grants and innovation programs offer financial support to entrepreneurs aiming to develop AI technologies. These programs not only provide funding but also offer resources and mentorship to help startups navigate the challenges of bringing AI products to market. By tapping into these funding sources, entrepreneurs can accelerate their growth and establish a strong presence in the AI landscape.

Success stories of AI entrepreneurs provide both inspiration and practical lessons. Take, for example, a startup that disrupted the logistics industry by using AI to optimize supply chain operations. By predicting demand and automating processes, they reduced costs and improved efficiency, setting a new standard for the industry. Another example is an AI-driven platform that transformed personalized marketing through real-time data analysis and targeted campaigns. These pioneers faced challenges but persevered, leveraging AI's capabilities to overcome obstacles and achieve remarkable success. Their journeys highlight the importance of innovation, adaptability, and a willingness to embrace new technologies. They also underscore the value of learning from setbacks and using those experiences to refine strategies and enhance offerings.

7.6 Networking in the AI Field: Building Professional Connections

Networking is characterized by active discussions and collaboration among professionals. It fosters the exchange of ideas and information, creating valuable connections that can lead to opportunities and advancements in technology. Building relationships with professionals and mentors opens doors to opportunities that might otherwise remain hidden. It's about more than exchanging business cards; it's about forging connections that can guide your career and spark innovation. Through networking, you can access job openings, gain insights into industry trends, and find mentors who can offer invaluable guidance. These relationships are the lifelines that keep you plugged into our ever-evolving world, where staying ahead is as much about who you know as what you know.

Effective networking strategies can significantly enhance your presence in the community. Attending conferences and industry events is a key strategy. These gatherings are where thought leaders share groundbreaking ideas and where you can engage in discussions that challenge and expand your thinking. They provide a platform to meet industry experts, potential collaborators, and peers who share your interests. Engaging with professionals on platforms like LinkedIn is another crucial strategy. LinkedIn is the digital equivalent of a networking dinner, where you can connect with professionals, join discussions, and showcase your expertise. It allows you to maintain relationships formed at conferences and continue conversations that might lead to collaborative projects or career opportunities.

Networking today is not confined to traditional settings. Online and offline opportunities abound, offering flexibility to connect in ways that suit your lifestyle and preferences. Participating in webinars and virtual meetups provides access to a global community without the constraints of geography. These online events often feature experts who share insights and trends, allowing you to learn and engage from the comfort of your own home. They are fantastic opportunities to ask questions and participate in discussions that deepen your understanding of a particular subject. On the other hand, joining clubs and local meetups offers the chance for face-to-face interaction, fostering deeper connections through shared experiences. These in-person gatherings provide a supportive environment where you can exchange ideas, collaborate on projects, and build a network of local enthusiasts.

The benefits of networking extend far beyond immediate career opportunities. Networking can lead to career advancement and personal growth by providing insights into industry trends and emerging technologies. These connections often become sounding boards for ideas, helping you refine your thoughts and strategies. They keep you informed about shifts in the industry, allowing you to anticipate changes and adapt. Additionally, mentors found through networking offer personal guidance that can be transformative. Whether it's advice on navigating a challenging project or insights into career progression, these mentors provide a wealth of knowledge and experience. Their support can be pivotal in making informed decisions and achieving your goals.

Networking is about building a community of support where shared knowledge and collaboration drive progress. It's about leveraging these connections to enhance your career and contribute to the field. As you engage with a community, you'll find that the relationships you build are as enriching as the knowledge you gain. These connections are the threads that weave together the fabric of your professional life, providing support, inspiration, and opportunities to grow. Whether through a chance meeting at a conference or a virtual discussion that sparks a new idea, networking is the key to unlocking the potential within you and your field.

8

The Future of AI and Continuous Learning

8.1 Future Trends in AI: What's on the Horizon

Consider a living room equipped with various smart devices that connect and communicate with one another. These devices can automatically adjust the lighting, temperature, and music based on user preferences and environmental conditions. This scenario reflects the current advancements in AI technology and its ability to enhance daily living through automation and improved connectivity. As we look ahead, we see AI intertwining with emerging technologies, creating a landscape where innovation and everyday life converge in ways we are only beginning to understand. The rapid pace of change in AI makes it crucial to stay informed and adapt to the advancements on the horizon.

One of the most transformative developments in AI is the rise of quantum computing. Unlike traditional computers, which process information in bits, quantum computers use qubits that can represent and process data in complex ways. This capability opens up unprecedented potential for AI, especially in solving problems that are currently too complex for classical computers. Imagine AI systems that can process vast datasets with incredible speed, leading to breakthroughs in fields like cryptography, drug discovery, and climate modeling. Although quantum computing is still in its nascent stages, its integration with AI promises to revolutionize how we approach complex computational challenges.

Alongside quantum computing, the Internet of Things (IoT) is another domain where AI is making significant strides. IoT refers to the network of physical devices that connect and exchange data, from smart home gadgets to industrial sensors. AI plays a pivotal role in analyzing this data, enabling devices to learn from interactions and improve their functionality. For instance, smart thermostats use AI to learn your heating preferences, optimizing energy use while maintaining comfort. As IoT devices become more prevalent, AI will enhance their capabilities, leading to smarter cities, more efficient transportation systems, and improved environmental monitoring.

AI's reach extends beyond Earth, venturing into the realm of space exploration. AI algorithms assist in analyzing satellite data, optimizing spacecraft operations, and even identifying exoplanets. With AI, space agencies can process the immense volume of data collected from telescopes and satellites more efficiently, uncovering insights about our universe. AI aids in autonomous navigation for space probes, allowing them to adapt to new environments and make decisions without human intervention. This ability is crucial for missions exploring distant worlds, where communication delays make real-time human control impractical.

In personalized medicine and genomics, AI is poised to revolutionize healthcare. By analyzing genetic information and patient data, AI can help develop tailored treatment plans that consider individual differences. This approach shifts medical practices from reactive to proactive, focusing on prevention and personalized care. AI's ability to identify patterns in genetic data can lead to breakthroughs in understanding diseases and developing targeted therapies. However, this transformation also raises ethical concerns about data privacy and the potential for bias in AI recommendations, requiring careful consideration and regulation.

Speaking of bias and privacy, the growing influence of AI also brings ethical and societal challenges. As AI becomes more integrated into decision-making processes, questions arise about accountability and transparency. In geopolitical contexts, AI-driven technologies can influence power dynamics, necessitating thoughtful regulation to ensure equitable use. The EU's Artificial Intelligence Act and China's proactive AI regulations exemplify the varied approaches to governance, aiming to balance innovation with societal welfare. Addressing AI's impact on job markets and economic structures is another concern. While AI creates new opportunities, it also disrupts traditional industries, highlighting the need for policies that support workforce transitions and skill development.

Predictive analytics, powered by AI, is becoming a cornerstone of strategic decision-making. By analyzing trends and forecasting outcomes, AI helps organizations anticipate changes and adapt proactively. In climate change modeling, AI-driven analytics offer insights into future environmental conditions, informing policy decisions and sustainability efforts. Similarly, businesses use AI to predict market trends, enabling them to respond to consumer demands and shifts in the economy with agility. These capabilities underscore AI's potential to transform how we plan for the future, encouraging data-driven approaches to complex challenges.

Interactive Element: Exploring AI's Potential

Consider how AI might transform a field you're interested in. Reflect on potential applications, ethical challenges, and societal impacts. Write a short paragraph or brainstorm your thoughts and share them with a friend or colleague to spark discussion.

8.2 Lifelong Learning with AI: Resources and Strategies

Picture a classroom not bound by walls or geography, where AI tailors the learning experience to fit your individual pace and preferences. This is the promise of lifelong learning in the age of AI—a dynamic, personalized educational journey uniquely suited to each learner. AI is democratizing education, making it accessible to anyone with an internet connection. No longer do you need to attend an elite university to gain specialized knowledge; AI brings the classroom to your home, offering a wealth of resources and tools designed to cater to your learning style.

Online platforms like Coursera and edX have revolutionized how we approach learning. They provide courses from top universities and institutions worldwide, offering everything from beginner programming to advanced machine learning, and the same goes for many other fields. These platforms let you learn at your own pace, fitting education into your schedule, whether you're a busy professional or a student. AI-focused MOOCs (Massive Open Online Courses) and certification programs allow you to gain valuable skills in AI, equipping you for the future job market. These courses are often designed by industry experts, ensuring that you learn the latest techniques and tools used in the field today.

For those who prefer a more self-directed approach, setting learning goals and tracking progress is crucial. Start by identifying the skills you want to develop, then break them down into smaller, manageable tasks. Use AI-powered learning assistants and study tools to guide your journey. These tools can recommend resources, keep track of your progress, and even quiz you on what you've learned, reinforcing your knowledge and ensuring you stay on track. By taking control of your education, you can tailor your learning experience to suit your personal and professional goals, making it a more rewarding and effective process.

Community-based learning and collaboration offer another layer of support and enrichment. Participating in AI study groups and collaborative projects allows you to learn from peers, share insights, and tackle challenges together. These communities provide a supportive environment where you can ask questions, share your experiences, and learn from others' perspectives. For example, engaging in hackathons and AI challenges can also boost your skills, offering hands-on experience in problem-solving and innovation. These events simulate real-world scenarios, requiring you to apply your knowledge creatively and collaboratively. They are excellent opportunities to network with like-minded individuals, build your portfolio, and demonstrate your capabilities to potential employers.

AI is more than just a tool for learning; it's a partner in your educational journey. It adapts to your learning style, providing personalized feedback and recommendations to enhance your understanding. Whether you're exploring new topics or deepening your expertise, AI helps you stay engaged and motivated. In this ever-evolving field, continuous learning is not just beneficial—it's necessary. By embracing AI's potential in education, you equip yourself with the skills needed to thrive in an increasingly complex world, prepared to face the challenges and opportunities that lie ahead.

8.3 Innovation and Creativity: The Role of AI in New Ideas

In the vibrant landscape of creativity, AI emerges as a powerful ally, pushing the boundaries of what's possible across various domains. Take music composition, for instance. AI tools like AIVA and OpenAI's MuseNet can generate original compositions, blending genres and styles to create unique music pieces. These AI systems analyze thousands of compositions, learning patterns and structures to craft innovative and familiar melodies. Musicians use these AI-generated pieces as foundations, adding their flair to create something truly original. The collaboration between AI and human creativity leads to music that resonates on multiple levels, showcasing a blend of technology and artistry.

Visual arts also benefit from AI's creative potential. Artists leverage AI to transform traditional art forms, using algorithms to generate new styles and patterns. Tools like DeepArt and RunwayML allow artists to experiment with colors and textures, producing works that would be challenging to achieve by hand. AI's ability to process and reinterpret vast amounts of visual data enables artists to explore new dimensions in their work, pushing creative boundaries. In writing, AI-generated prompts inspire authors, offering fresh perspectives and ideas that can lead to unexpected narrative twists. Writers use AI as a collaborative partner, sparking creativity and helping overcome writer's block by suggesting plot developments and character arcs.

The potential for collaboration extends beyond individual artists to entire industries, where AI plays a critical role in co-creating art and design. In architecture, AI aids in generating innovative building designs, optimizing space, and enhancing functionality. Tools like Autodesk's Generative Design help architects explore multiple design options, considering factors such as materials, lighting, and environmental impact. This collaboration leads to structures that are not only aesthetically pleasing but also efficient and sustainable. Similarly, in fashion, AI assists designers in predicting trends, creating new patterns, and even automating certain aspects of garment production. AI platforms analyze consumer data, helping designers tailor collections that resonate with current tastes and preferences, thus staying ahead in a competitive market.

In the business realm, AI drives innovation by transforming how companies develop products and conduct market research. Businesses use AI to analyze consumer behavior, identifying trends and preferences that inform product development. This data-driven approach allows companies to create products that meet consumer needs more effectively. AI also automates innovation processes, streamlining research and development activities. By analyzing vast datasets, AI uncovers insights that might be overlooked by human researchers, leading to new opportunities and competitive advantages. Companies that leverage AI in their innovation processes often find themselves at the forefront of their industries, able to respond quickly to changing market dynamics.

Several case studies highlight AI's transformative impact on creativity. In fashion, AI-designed collections have graced runways, blending technology with traditional craftsmanship to produce garments that are both cutting-edge and wearable. Exhibitions showcasing these collections demonstrate AI's ability to enhance creative processes, offering designers new tools and techniques. In the music industry, AI-assisted albums push the boundaries of what's possible, allowing artists to explore new sounds and compositions. Performances combining AI-assisted music with live musicians create immersive experiences where technology and artistry converge to captivate audiences. These examples illustrate AI's role as a catalyst for creativity, enabling artists and businesses to explore new frontiers and redefine their fields.

The intersection of AI and creativity is not just about producing new works; it's about expanding the possibilities of human imagination. By partnering with AI, creators can explore new ideas, challenge conventions, and innovate in ways previously unimaginable. AI doesn't replace human creativity; it enhances it, providing tools and insights that unlock new levels of potential. This synergy between humans and machines fosters a dynamic exchange of ideas, where technology amplifies the creative process and opens doors to endless possibilities. As AI continues to evolve, its impact on creativity and innovation will only grow, offering new paths for exploration and expression across diverse fields.

8.4 Assessing AI Applications: Cost vs. Benefit Analysis

When considering an AI investment, it's akin to planning a major home renovation. You must weigh the costs against the potential benefits to ensure that your project not only adds value but also aligns with your goals and resources. The initial setup and ongoing maintenance of AI systems can be substantial. You might face expenses for hardware and software licenses, as well as hiring skilled personnel to manage these systems. These upfront costs are critical to understand, as they set the foundation for your AI infrastructure. Beyond setup, maintenance can also be a significant factor, involving regular updates, troubleshooting, and system enhancements. It's similar to keeping a car running smoothly; neglecting maintenance can lead to costly breakdowns that disrupt operations.

Calculating the return on investment (ROI) is a vital step in assessing the viability of AI applications. ROI involves not just measuring financial returns but also considering efficiency gains and improved outcomes. For example, an AI-driven customer service system might reduce operational costs by handling routine inquiries, allowing human agents to focus on complex issues. This shift can improve customer satisfaction and lead to greater loyalty, indirectly boosting revenue. The goal is to ensure that the benefits outweigh the costs, leading to a net positive impact on your bottom line. Evaluating ROI requires a comprehensive approach, considering both tangible and intangible benefits, and often necessitates a long-term perspective to fully appreciate the value AI can bring.

Balancing innovation with practicality is crucial when integrating AI into your operations. It's tempting to pursue cutting-edge technologies, but overinvestment in unproven AI solutions can lead to wasted resources and unmet expectations. Consider the alignment of AI initiatives with your organizational goals. If a new AI tool promises to revolutionize your processes, ensure it fits within your broader strategy and that the potential benefits justify the investment. This alignment ensures that AI acts as an enabler rather than a distraction, supporting your core objectives and enhancing overall effectiveness. The excitement of innovation must be tempered with a pragmatic understanding of how AI fits into the existing framework and contributes to long-term success.

Risk assessment and management are integral to any AI investment. Identifying potential security vulnerabilities in AI systems is essential, as these systems often handle sensitive data. Implementing robust security measures and protocols can mitigate risks, protect against breaches, and ensure compliance with regulations. Developing contingency plans is also a smart strategy to manage potential AI project failures. Just as a business would prepare for unexpected market shifts, having a backup plan for AI initiatives can minimize disruption and allow for rapid recovery. These plans should include steps for addressing technical issues, reallocating resources, and maintaining continuity in operations. By anticipating challenges and preparing for them, you can navigate the complexities of AI integration with greater confidence.

Examining real-world examples provides valuable insights into the cost-benefit dynamics of AI investments. In retail, AI-powered supply chain optimization has demonstrated significant benefits. By analyzing data on inventory levels, demand forecasts, and supplier performance, AI systems can streamline operations, reducing waste and improving efficiency. This optimization often translates into cost savings and enhanced customer satisfaction. Conversely, some AI-driven marketing campaigns have not met expectations. Despite the promise of personalized customer interactions, a lack of integration with existing systems or inadequate data quality can lead to ineffective campaigns. These cases highlight the importance of comprehensive planning and execution in AI investments, emphasizing the need for a strategic approach that considers all factors.

> *Case Study: AI in Retail Supply Chain Optimization*
> *A leading retailer implemented AI to enhance its supply chain. The AI system analyzed sales patterns and optimized inventory levels, reducing stockouts and excess inventory. This approach led to a 15% decrease in holding costs and improved service levels, demonstrating the tangible benefits of AI investment. This case underscores the potential for AI to drive efficiency and profitability when aligned with strategic goals.*

A thoughtful approach is required when evaluating AI investments. It involves understanding costs, estimating returns, balancing innovation with practicality, and managing risks effectively. By learning from successful and unsuccessful examples, businesses can make informed decisions that leverage AI's transformative potential while safeguarding their interests.

8.5 Preparing for the Future: Adapting to AI-Driven Changes

As we stand on the brink of a new era, AI is poised to redefine industries, reshaping how they operate and deliver value. In manufacturing, the shift towards Industry 4.0 epitomizes this transformation, integrating AI with automation and data exchange to create smart factories. These factories employ AI to enhance production efficiency, predict maintenance needs, and optimize supply chains. Imagine a factory floor where machines communicate seamlessly, anticipating failures before they occur and autonomously adjusting processes to maintain peak performance. This level of sophistication reduces downtime, lowers costs, and boosts productivity, enabling manufacturers to meet changing consumer demands with agility.

In healthcare, AI's influence is equally transformative, fundamentally altering delivery and patient care. AI systems analyze vast datasets, identifying patterns and insights that aid in diagnosing diseases and personalizing treatments. Picture a scenario where AI assists doctors in diagnosing conditions with unprecedented accuracy, considering genetic, environmental, and lifestyle factors to craft individualized care plans. This approach not only improves patient outcomes but also enhances the efficiency of healthcare delivery, reducing waiting times and optimizing resource allocation. As these technologies integrate into daily operations, healthcare providers must navigate challenges, including ensuring data privacy and addressing ethical considerations, to fully realize AI's potential.

To thrive amid these AI-driven changes, adopting a proactive mindset is crucial. This begins with embracing a culture of innovation and continuous improvement, where organizations and individuals alike actively seek opportunities to leverage AI for growth. Encouraging experimentation and fostering a willingness to adapt can lead to breakthroughs and novel solutions. Moreover, cultivating adaptability and resilience prepares you to navigate uncertainties and capitalize on emerging trends. In a rapidly changing landscape, the ability to pivot and learn from experiences becomes invaluable, enabling you to remain agile and competitive.

Developing skills and competencies that align with an AI-driven future is key to staying relevant. Critical thinking and problem-solving skills are paramount, allowing you to interpret AI insights and make informed decisions. In an era where AI handles routine tasks, these skills distinguish you, enabling you to tackle complex challenges that require human judgment. Additionally, emotional intelligence and human-AI collaboration skills become increasingly important. As AI takes on more roles, understanding how to work alongside these systems and leverage their capabilities enhances productivity and innovation.

As organizations prepare for AI adoption, developing AI literacy programs for employees is a strategic priority. These programs demystify AI concepts, equipping employees with the knowledge to engage with AI tools effectively. By aligning organizational structures with AI-driven workflows, companies can streamline operations and enhance decision-making processes. This alignment involves integrating AI into strategic planning and ensuring that teams have the resources and support needed to leverage AI effectively. Encouraging cross-functional collaboration and fostering a culture of learning further supports successful AI integration, enabling organizations to harness AI's potential to drive innovation and growth.

9

Conclusion

As you reach the end of this journey through the landscape of artificial intelligence, take a moment to reflect on the transformative potential you've explored. We've journeyed from the basics of AI, understanding its core principles, to delving into the diverse applications that touch nearly every aspect of our lives. From assisting in daily tasks to revolutionizing industries like healthcare and education, AI stands as a versatile ally in our modern world.

Throughout the chapters, we've explored how AI can enhance personal productivity, streamline professional tasks, and even offer emotional support. You've seen how AI tools like ChatGPT can turn routine tasks into efficient processes, freeing you to focus on what truly matters. In creative fields, AI has emerged as a partner, offering new avenues for expression and innovation. In the industrial realm, its impact on automation and efficiency is undeniable, promising safer and smarter solutions.

The key takeaway from this exploration is empowerment. AI is not an abstract concept reserved for experts. It's an accessible tool that you can harness to simplify your life and amplify your potential. Whether you're a student, professional, or entrepreneur, AI offers opportunities to enhance your skillset, optimize your workflow, and innovate within your field. The knowledge you've gained equips you to leverage AI with confidence and creativity.

But the journey with AI doesn't stop here. The field is constantly evolving, with new advancements emerging at a rapid pace. Embrace the mindset of a lifelong learner. Stay curious and open to the possibilities that AI continues to present. Engage with online courses, participate in AI communities, and follow industry trends to keep your knowledge fresh and relevant. As AI shapes the future, your proactive approach will ensure you remain at the forefront of these changes.

Now, it's time for action. Consider how you can implement AI into your daily routine. Start small—explore AI tools for time management or creative projects. Experiment with AI-driven platforms to learn new skills or optimize your work processes. The key is to integrate AI gradually, building your confidence and understanding as you go. Share your experiences with peers, and encourage others to explore AI's potential alongside you.

Reflecting on the vision behind this book, I aimed to demystify AI and make it approachable for everyone. By breaking down complex concepts into simple, relatable terms, I hope to have eased any intimidation surrounding AI. My goal was to equip you with the knowledge and tools to confidently navigate the AI landscape, transforming potential challenges into exciting opportunities.

I want to express my heartfelt gratitude for embarking on this journey with me. Your willingness to explore and learn is what drives me to share this knowledge. Remember, you're not alone on this path. A community of learners and innovators surrounds you, ready to support and inspire.

As you close this book, take with you the empowerment to explore, the courage to innovate, and the curiosity to continue learning. AI is a tool, a partner, and a catalyst for change. Use it wisely and creatively. The future is bright, and with AI by your side, you're equipped to shape it in meaningful, impactful ways.

Keeping the Journey Alive

Now that you have everything you need to master AI learning, explore tools, and optimize your career, it's your turn to inspire others.

By sharing your honest opinion of *AI for Beginners: Master AI Learning With Easy-to-Understand Tool Selection, Hands-On Practice, and Career Optimization Insights* on Amazon, you'll guide curious readers—just like you—to the resources they need to unlock the exciting possibilities of AI.

Your review doesn't just help readers find this book; it keeps the passion for learning AI alive. Every review is like a spark, lighting the way for someone else who's eager to learn and grow.

Thank you for helping me in this mission. Together, we're building a community of learners, creators, and innovators.

Click here to leave your review on Amazon.

With gratitude,

Eden Wilder

References

1. GeeksforGeeks. (n.d.). **AI vs traditional programming - What's the difference?** https://www.geeksforgeeks.org/what-is-artificial-intelligence-ai-and-how-does-it-differ-from-traditional-programming/
2. LinkedIn Pulse. (n.d.). **From Siri to Alexa: A brief history of conversational AI and more.** https://www.linkedin.com/pulse/from-siri-alexa-brief-history-conversational-ai-raghu
3. Pathmind. (n.d.). **A beginner's guide to neural networks and deep learning.** https://wiki.pathmind.com/neural-network
4. CNBC. (2023, December 24). **The top 10 AI tools of 2023, and how to use them to make more money.** https://www.cnbc.com/2023/12/24/the-top-10-ai-tools-of-2023-and-how-to-use-them-to-make-more-money.html
5. Team GPT. (2024). **5 best ChatGPT use cases in 2024 [Prompts included].** https://team-gpt.com/blog/chatgpt-use-cases/
6. Zapier. (2024). **The 8 best AI scheduling assistants in 2024.** https://zapier.com/blog/best-ai-scheduling/
7. MDPI. (2024). **Ethical considerations in artificial intelligence interventions.** https://www.mdpi.com/2076-0760/13/7/381
8. Simplilearn. (n.d.). **How to use ChatGPT for beginners.** https://www.simplilearn.com/tutorials/chatgpt-tutorial/chatgpt-for-beginners
9. ZDNet. (2024). **The best AI image generators of 2024: Tested and**

reviewed. https://www.zdnet.com/article/best-ai-image-generator/

10. McKinsey & Company. (n.d.). **Generative AI in healthcare: Adoption trends and what's next.** https://www.mckinsey.com/industries/healthcare/our-insights/generative-ai-in-healthcare-adoption-trends-and-whats-next
11. Vision Platform. (n.d.). **Advancements and applications in unmanned aerial vehicles.** https://visionplatform.ai/artificial-intelligence-drones/
12. Nature. (n.d.). **Robotics: Ethics of artificial intelligence.** https://www.nature.com/articles/521415a
13. Brookings Institution. (n.d.). **The evolving safety and policy challenges of self-driving cars.** https://www.brookings.edu/articles/the-evolving-safety-and-policy-challenges-of-self-driving-cars/
14. OECD. (n.d.). **AI principles.** https://www.oecd.org/en/topics/sub-issues/ai-principles.html
15. Princeton Dialogues on AI and Ethics. (n.d.). **Case studies.** https://aiethics.princeton.edu/case-studies/
16. MIT Sloan. (n.d.). **Unmasking the bias in facial recognition algorithms.** https://mitsloan.mit.edu/ideas-made-to-matter/unmasking-bias-facial-recognition-algorithms
17. IEEE Spectrum. (n.d.). **AI experts speak: Memorable quotes from Spectrum's AI.** https://spectrum.ieee.org/artificial-intelligence-quotes
18. AutoGPT. (n.d.). **The best 23 AI newsletters to keep in your inbox.** https://autogpt.net/the-top-10-best-ai-newsletters-to-keep-in-your-inbox/
19. MakeUseOf. (n.d.). **9 communities for beginners to learn about AI tools.** https://www.makeuseof.com/online-communities-to-learn-about-ai/

20. Gu, E. (n.d.). **Teaching designers AI literacy: Practical exercises.** Medium. https://arteliers.medium.com/teaching-designers-ai-literacy-c48e26689f7a
21. Wells, R. (2024, March 31). **5 AI resume builders you should try in 2024.** Forbes. https://www.forbes.com/sites/rachelwells/2024/03/31/5-ai-resume-builders-you-should-try-in-2024/
22. ClickUp. (2024). **10 educational AI tools for students in 2024.** https://clickup.com/blog/ai-tools-for-students/
23. University of Texas at San Antonio. (n.d.). **The growing demand for AI skills and expertise in the job market.** https://www.utsa.edu/pace/news/growing-demand-for-ai-skills-and-expertise-in-the-job-market.html
24. AIM Research. (n.d.). **10 generative AI success stories: How businesses transformed their operations.** https://aimresearch.co/market-industry/10-generative-ai-success-stories-how-businesses-transformed-their-operations
25. IBM. (n.d.). **The top artificial intelligence trends.** https://www.ibm.com/think/insights/artificial-intelligence-trends
26. PMC. (n.d.). **Artificial intelligence (AI) in personalized medicine: AI applications.** https://pmc.ncbi.nlm.nih.gov/articles/PMC10617817/
27. Forbes Technology Council. (2024, June 25). **AI and the democratization of knowledge.** Forbes. https://www.forbes.com/councils/forbestechcouncil/2024/06/25/ai-and-the-democratization-of-knowledge/
28. Forbes Technology Council. (2024, October 22). **How AI generative models are transforming creativity: Real-world case studies in art, music, and writing.** Forbes. https://www.forbes.com/councils/forbestechcouncil/2024/10/22/how-ai-generative-models-are-transforming-creativity-real-world-case-studies-in-art-music-and-writing/

www.ingramcontent.com/pod-product-compliance
Lightning Source LLC
LaVergne TN
LVHW022006200926
848481LV00007B/2251